The Goddess Is in the Details is a champion of common sense. Advanced Witches can focus on the small and big stuff concerning the witchy lifestyle. What I enjoyed best were the incantations: fresh verses, good rhymes.

Z Budapest, author of *The Holy Book of Women's Mysteries* and *Summoning the Fates*

Another Witch once told me what sets us apart from others is our capability to see the magickal in the mundane. Deborah Blake has created a practical method of weaving the spiritual into the daily chores of the mundane world in which we must live. Easy to read and easy to implement, *The Goddess Is in the Details* is a reference and a comfort for any Witch seeking new practices to bring Pagan spirituality into every part of our lives.

Edain McCoy, author of *Advanced Witchcraft, The Witch's Coven,* and *If You Want to Be a Witch*

Getting back to our roots (pun intended!) and practicing our creed every day is the goal of *The Goddess Is in the Details*. Fun to read and chock-full of sensible advice, Deborah Blake's new book should find a place in every Pagan's library. Whether you are a beginning Pagan just finding your way or an experienced elder in the tradition, you will find something of comfort, enjoyment, and practicality in this book. With its warm and intimate tone, it inspires the reader and reminds us that our hearts and our hearths are the abodes of our deities: our gods and goddesses are always with us.

Denise Dumars, author of *Be Blessed: Daily Devotions for Busy Wiccans and Pagans*

Everyday Witchcraft

About the Author

Deborah Blake is a Wiccan high priestess who has been leading an eclectic group, Blue Moon Circle, since Beltane 2004. She is the author of *The Goddess Is in the Details* (Llewellyn, 2009) and *The Witch's Broom* (Llewellyn, 2014), among others, and she has written a number of articles for Pagan publications.

When not writing, Deborah manages the Artisans' Guild, a cooperative shop she founded with a friend in 1999, and works as a jewelry maker, tarot reader, ordained minister, and intuitive energy healer. She lives in a 100-year-old farmhouse in rural upstate New York with five cats who supervise all her activities, both magickal and mundane.

Deborah Blake

Everyday Witchcraft

Making Time
for Spirit in
a Too-Busy
World

Llewellyn Publications

WOODBURY, MINNESOTA

FIRST EDITION
Ninth Printing, 2022

Book design by Rebecca Zins
Cover design by Lisa Novak
Cover illustration by Jennifer Hewitson
Salt doll outline on page 101 by Llewellyn Art Department

Llewellyn Publications is a registered trademark of Llewellyn Worldwide Ltd.

Library of Congress Cataloging-in-Publication Data
Blake, Deborah, 1960–
  Everyday witchcraft : making time for spirit in a too-busy world / Deborah Blake.—first edition.
     pages   cm
  Includes bibliographical references.
  ISBN 978-0-7387-4218-2
  1. Witchcraft. I. Title.
  BF1571.B53 2015
  133.4'3—dc23
                                                          2014042208

Llewellyn Worldwide does not participate in, endorse, or have any authority or responsibility concerning private business transactions between our authors and the public.

All mail addressed to the author is forwarded, but the publisher cannot, unless specifically instructed by the author, give out an address or phone number.

Any Internet references contained in this work are current at publication time, but the publisher cannot guarantee that a specific location will continue to be maintained. Please refer to the publisher's website for links to authors' websites and other sources.

Llewellyn Publications
A Division of Llewellyn Worldwide Ltd.
2143 Wooddale Drive
Woodbury, MN 55125-2989
www.llewellyn.com

Printed in the United States of America

To Samhain:
tiny in size but large of heart,
whose presence in my life was a gift
for every day I had her. All cats are wonderful,
but few as wonderful as this one.
Walk in peace with the gods.

CONTENTS

CONTENTS

CONTENTS

Acknowledgments

For Blue Moon Circle: without you, these books would be much shorter (and my life much emptier)!

For Elysia Gallo and Becky Zins: without you, these books wouldn't be nearly as good.

A BIG HUGE thanks to all the lovely and talented authors who took the time to write a contribution for this book, sharing their own approaches and ideas so you weren't stuck just listening to me. These are some of the greatest names in modern Witchcraft today, and I am grateful beyond measure that they were so enthusiastic about being a part of this book.

And for everyone who loved The Goddess Is in the Details and told me so—this one's for you, my readers. You people ROCK.

Living Your Best Magickal and Mundane Life

Once upon a time, I wrote a book called *The Goddess Is in the Details: Wisdom for the Everyday Witch*. I'd written two books before that one and have written many since, but there was something special about *The Goddess Is in the Details*. Of course, I hope that there is something special about all my books, but this one seemed to hit a chord with a lot of people.

Goddess has, at the time of this writing, gone on to have six printings, more than any of my other books. I get more notes and emails from readers telling me that *The Goddess Is in the Details* has helped them, touched them, and inspired them, and I must confess, it is my favorite too. (Shhh…don't tell the other books.)

So what is it about this particular book that made it stand out? After all, I've written spellbooks and ritual books, books for covens, and books that help people practice Witchcraft without spending a lot of money. What is different about *The Goddess Is in the Details*?

I think the answer lies in my intent when I wrote the book. I wanted to go beyond the usual "101" books, the ritual and spellworking basics—not that these kinds of books aren't wonderful and useful; I have shelves filled with them. But living a magickal life isn't just about casting spells, chanting under the full moon, and celebrating the sabbats. To me, living your best magickal and mundane life means moving beyond the separation between the two; in fact, if you are truly going to walk your talk as a Witch, there can be no separation.

This doesn't mean that you have to go around telling everyone you meet that you're a Witch. What it does mean is finding ways to integrate your spiritual beliefs as a Pagan with your day-to-day life. And that was what *The Goddess Is in the Details* was all about. From home and family to mindful eating to dealing with times of crisis, I tried to come up with suggestions that were meaningful but also reasonably fast and easy to fit into most people's already overwhelming demands on their time and energy. From the response to the book, I'm guessing that I succeeded.

So—why write another book with the same basic theme?

Well, I might have left a few things out the first time. After all, you can only fit so much into any one book without making it so large it would constitute your daily exercise just to pick it up. And frankly, I've learned a few things since then and changed the way I view other things.

At the time I write this, I have been practicing Witchcraft for almost seventeen years: five-and-a-half years studying with my first high priestess, a year as a solitary after I left that group, and then ten-plus years as high priestess to my own group, Blue Moon Circle. Needless to say, over that time things in my life—and in me—have changed, and how I practice my Craft has changed with them. Even Blue Moon Circle has changed, fluctuating over the years from the three core people it started with, up to as many as eight or nine, and back down to six.

I've also made connections over that time with many of my readers, some of whom have asked me questions that never got answered in any of my other books. So right about the time I signed the contract for my first published novels and said to myself I *guess that's it for the nonfiction*, a little voice in my head said, "Wait! There's one more book you have to write first."

Yes, ma'am.

Never ignore that voice.

Which brings us here, to this book. It is, in theory, a follow-up of sorts to *The Goddess Is in the Details*. But it is also a book that stands by itself, and you certainly don't need to have ever read anything else of mine for this book to work for you. I cover some things in both books (in different ways), and some things only in this one.

The main thing these books have in common is their intent to help you live your best possible magickal and mundane life. We all walk very different paths as Pagans and Witches, and what is right for one person won't be right for the next. But my aim is to make it easier for you to find and follow the path that is right for you, integrating spirit and magick and heart into your everyday tasks as you walk it.

Because isn't that what all of us really want? To be our best selves, to live our happiest and most fulfilled lives, and to walk our paths with grace and wisdom, with occasional stops along the way to dance with joy?

I hope this book helps you to achieve that, and I am honored that you are bringing me along on the path with you.

Blessed be,

Deborah

A Note on Names

Writing a book about Witchcraft can be kind of tricky. There are Wiccans and Witches and Pagans—oh my!—not to mention the folks who follow some kind of spiritual path that is more or less one of the above but doesn't fall under any of those categories or who prefer not to put any name at all on what they believe. And then there are the people who are curious or open-minded or interested in some aspects of a Witchcraft practice but not others.

Yoinks.

I use the terms *Pagan* and *Witch* pretty much interchangeably most of the time, mostly for ease of use. Feel free to mentally substitute whatever label makes you the most comfortable, and just know that in most cases, I'm talking about "you, the reader" no matter what name I use.

Maybe I should have just used Bubba. You know, like: *To be a well-rounded Bubba, you should always bathe before rituals.* (Snicker.) Never mind. I guess I'll just stick with Witch and Pagan.

Witchcraft in the Modern World

Witchcraft today is different than it was in the distant past, when most of the people we would call Witches might not even have used that name for themselves. They were herbalists and magic users and goddess worshipers, but they led very different lives than the lives we lead today. Their Witchcraft may be where ours gets its roots, but it was not our Witchcraft.

The truth of the matter is that Witchcraft today is an ever-evolving landscape. From the time of Witchcraft's return to open view in the 1950s with such notables as Gerald Gardner, modern Witchcraft has changed and reinvented itself many times, in many ways. It has gone from secretive covens with strict rules and degree systems to a feminist celebration of a forgotten goddess to an eclectic hodge-podge of Pagan origins ranging from Norse to Egyptian to Native American.

All of these variations still exist, along with countless others, and all of them are just as valid as whatever it was our ancient predecessors practiced. So how do you know if you are a Witch—and if you *are* a Witch, what kind of Witch are you?

Some of the folks reading this book will already have the answers to those questions. Others won't care, and that's just fine. You certainly don't *need* to know if you are a Witch or not, or what particular path you will be following, in order to use this book.

On the other hand, since the goal of this book is to help people integrate their spiritual beliefs with their everyday lives, you may find it useful to narrow things down a bit. At the very least, it is fascinating to see some of the various forms that modern Witchcraft takes.

I have been fortunate enough to attend a fabulous Pagan gathering that takes place every February in San Jose, California. Pantheacon is HUGE, with attendance that can reach well over two thousand people over the course of the three-and-a-half days it runs. There are amazing workshops, rituals, and musical performances, and you can often find many of your favorite witchy authors there. It is loud and bursting with energy, and sometimes overwhelming. It is also a fascinating place to simply people-watch because the convention is packed with every flavor of Pagan you could possibly imagine—and some you probably couldn't.

That's one of the things I love the most about being a Pagan. For the most part, we're a pretty accepting bunch. I'm not saying that there aren't Witches who criticize each other. Some folks are accused of being "fluffy bunny" Witches, meaning they are not serious enough, while others are scolded for being too radical or over the top; just like any other group of people, we have those who don't play well with others or who feel that their view is the Right One.

But for the most part, the Pagans I have met are happy to embrace each other (literally—they're a very huggy bunch, Pagans) no matter which form of Witchcraft they choose to practice.

If you're confused about what to call yourself, you're not alone. As I said, it can be kind of tricky to know what name to use in modern Witchcraft. The good news is, if you are talking about yourself, you can use whichever name you like best.

No Wrong Way

One of the great things about a modern Witchcraft practice is that there's no one right way to do it, which also means there is no wrong way.

Well, that's not strictly true, of course. If you are doing things that harm yourself or anyone else, I *personally* would consider that inappropriate at best and dangerous (to the spirit, if nothing else) at worst.

But this is not a "judging" religion, and you have to make those choices for yourself. Witchcraft is a spiritual practice that is based on personal responsibility, among other things. I discuss that more fully in *The Goddess Is in the Details*, so I'm not going to get into it here. Suffice it to say that, in general, Witches believe we are all responsible for our own actions and the consequences that follow them. No saying "the devil made me do it" or being absolved of your sins simply by confessing them. We all have to own our choices and live with the results.

In general, if you find a path that suits you—one that moves your life in positive directions and feeds your spirit—that is probably the right path for you. And unlike many other religions, the Pagan path is flexible; you can expect your practice to change over the course of the years as your life and your needs change.

Take me, for instance. My practice began with a group led by a woman who had been taught in a fairly formal Wiccan tradition and then practiced with a more eclectic bunch of folks along the way. By the time I joined her study group (she didn't call it a coven until many years down the road, although in many ways it functioned as one), she had evolved a practice that was what I would consider classical Wiccan in approach but without some of the more rigid aspects of some classical groups, like the First Degree, Second Degree, and Third Degree tiers of a Gardnerian coven. (Although she did have me do a "year and a day" of training before making my own dedication as a high priestess, which ended up taking longer—and not being done by her, but that's another story.)

For instance, when we did ritual, we had a male high priest and a female high priestess, and we used many of the elements found in traditional Wiccan rituals, including calling the quarters, lighting a red candle for the element of fire and a blue candle for the element of water, and so on (this is strictly a modern development, in case you didn't realize it; if the Witches of old used candles in their magickal work, they almost certainly used plain, uncolored ones).

If you read my books, you will see that I still use many of these elements in my own practice with others. I find the repetition of known patterns helps to establish a basis for a group working, and these are simple components that feel comfortable to me. You might say they make sense on a basic gut level.

However, as I have changed and evolved over the years, so has my Witchcraft practice. Within my own group, Blue Moon Circle, various members occasionally take turns leading rituals; this has happened more and more as other people grew in experience and confidence. Sometimes someone would introduce an element that we all liked better than the one I'd been using, so we'd adopt that new thing and add it to our repertoire.

For instance, as high priestess I usually cast the circle, and then we call the quarters individually, and then I invoke the Goddess (and the God, if it is a sabbat ritual and not the full moon). But one of the Blue Mooners found a lovely group invocation in which all the participants cast the circle, call the quarters, and invoke the Goddess in unison. We liked the energy of this so much, we often use it instead of the more traditional method. Change and evolution…it's a good thing.

My own personal practice has also changed. When I am on my own, my rituals tend to be more informal—I rarely cast a circle, for instance, beyond visualizing myself in sacred, protected space. Years of working magick have given me the ability to work without all the tools and patterns it used to take to achieve that level and depth of focus.

It's not that my initial form of practice was incorrect and what I do now is right or the other way around. My needs and style changed, so my practice changed with them. That is the beauty of a spiritual practice that can evolve as you do.

I used to refer to myself primarily as a Wiccan. I still use the term sometimes, depending on the person I am talking to; lots of non-Pagan folks are at least familiar with the term, and some find it less threatening than the term *Witch*, which has all sorts of misconceptions attached to it, from the ridiculous to the frightening.

On the other hand, I am among the people who believe that it is time to reclaim the word Witch with its more positive meanings, and I also feel, these days, that the broader "Witch" describes my current path better than calling myself a Wiccan (despite the fact that many of my practices are still very classic Wiccan in form), so I am much more likely to say that I am a Witch or, in a general religious discussion, that I am a Pagan.

None of these terms are wrong, and they all describe me in one way or another. But for the moment, at least, Witch seems to suit me best. As with all else, no doubt that is subject to change too.

If you are trying to decide what to call yourself, you may want to look at the general parameters of your spiritual practice, assuming you have one. If you tend toward the informal and are more likely to simply walk in the woods or stand under the moon than do any kind of ritual, you may want to call yourself a Pagan and leave it at that. If you follow a conventional Wiccan path or one of its many offshoots, then your choice is easy. For those who don't feel comfortable with the Wiccan name or image, or who don't follow the general "rules" (such as they are—Wicca is not terribly rule oriented—but, for instance, if you don't believe in "harm none," which not all Witches do) or if you like the more general nature of the word, you can always call yourself a Witch.

I like the way the word Witch connects us back through all the generations of those who went before us who harnessed the power of the elements and magick to improve their lives and deepen their connection with the natural world. But there is no wrong choice here. You can choose to call yourself anything you want, just as you can create the spiritual path that works best for your needs and is the best fit for your personality and your life.

....
Creating Your Personal Path

Once you've decided more or less which kind of Witch you are, you can work on creating the personal spiritual path that works best for you. For those who have already been practicing for years, you may already be well along that path, in which case you might want to assess whether or not it is still working for you (or ever really did).

For instance, if your spiritual path is mostly theoretical (you intend to do a full moon ritual every month but never seem to get around to it), you might want to consider ways to create a practice that will be easier to follow through on.

Here are some things to consider as you decide on or refine your spiritual path:

Needs and Desires

What are you looking to get from a spiritual practice? Do you want something that will be a comfort during difficult times or a way of making sense of the universe? Think about what it is you really want from whichever spiritual path you choose to walk.

For instance, I wanted to make a connection with deity. Through Wicca I was able to find the God and Goddess and really feel them in a way that never happened during my years as a Jew or going to the Unitarian Church or studying Buddhism. I also always have been drawn to the natural world, so having a spiritual path that was based on connection to earth, air, fire, water, and spirit just made sense to me.

You might want to take some time to think about what you are really hoping to find: faith, peace, hope, strength, energy, power, focus, direction, inspiration, love, acceptance, connection with nature or deity or your own inner spirit or others who believe as you do. Make a list of what you want to experience as you walk your path, then as you go through this book (and life in general) you can pick out the parts that will work best for your own spiritual path.

Personality and Preferences

Do you want a path that you will share with others or are you happier walking it alone? Do you want something with rules and predictable times of practice (like the full moon and the sabbats) or would you rather just do what moves you whenever you feel like it? It is important to find a path that suits your own personal inclinations, or you won't be happy with it. What's right for some other Witch won't necessarily be right for you.

I am someone who tends to spend a lot of time doing things on my own, so you would think that I would have chosen a solitary path. But, in fact, for all that I am a loner in most things, it turns out that I am a "group Witch." I do plenty of things on my own, of course, but I love the energy generated by a bunch of Witches all practicing together.

Not everyone can find people locally to practice with, even if that would be their preference. However, there are numerous online communities available these days or, as I did, you can find a few like-minded souls and start up your own group.

Freedom to Practice Openly

Much of a Witchcraft practice can be done in very subtle ways; kitchen witchery, for instance, can look just like making dinner. But the path you choose may depend in some part on how open you can be about your spiritual practices. If you share your home with people who aren't accepting of a Pagan religion, you may want to look at some of the options here that don't require an altar or any obvious Witchcraft tools.

Conversely, if you are raising your children as Pagans (as some of my friends are), you may want to find a path that makes it easy to include younger participants. There are plenty of "middle ground" options as well; for example, if you want to have an altar, tuck it away where no one can see it and just pull it out when you are alone.

Time and Energy

Let's be realistic: none of us has as much time and energy as we would like to be able to devote to our Witchcraft practices. For most of us, life is a matter of racing from one obligation to another and tending to jobs, significant others, children, pets, the house, and the million other things that fill our lives. It can be hard to find a moment to set aside for prayer, spellwork, or ritual. (Especially if you have kids!) It is easy for your spiritual practice to get pushed to last place on the to-do list we all struggle to accomplish every day.

On the other hand, if you are constantly drawing on the well of energy that comes from within, you have to do *something* to refill it or some day you will simply run out of gas and screech to a halt. So if you look at it another way, taking the time and energy for spiritual work is not so much an optional extra as it is a necessary ingredient to a well-balanced life.

Still, when looking at the kind of path you are trying to design (or reboot), be realistic about your expectations for time and energy to devote to the spiritual. If you will only be able to grab five minutes a day, you want to make them count. (See chapter 3's section on five-minute rituals for help with that.) If you intend to focus on magickal work for an hour or two twice a month, you may want to observe the full moons and new moons.

Each Witch's path is different, and each of us has the freedom to choose the kind of path that will best suit our needs and then follow it to the best of our abilities. For those of us who have been practicing for a long time, we also have the freedom (and some might say the responsibility) to change and adjust that path as our lives change and we learn and grow.

It can be hard to carve out time and focus for spiritual work. You have to decide that it is a priority and then follow up that commitment with action. No one is going to stand over you and make you do it. But hopefully the rest of this book will make it easier for you to integrate the spiritual practice you want into whatever kind of life you lead.

I will share with you something I figured out some years ago. Maybe it will give you the kind of "light bulb" moment it did me.

For a long time, I would look at certain Witches I knew and think, "That person has a special *something*. I don't know what it is, but I wish I could be more like her/him."

You know the kind of people I mean: the ones who seem to glow a little stronger and be a little bit more together and magickal. You don't know what it is about them, but in a crowd of Witches, these folks will always stand out. They aren't perfect; they still have problems and issues and bad days, just like the rest of us, but there is that "something" about them that draws you to them.

It took me a while, but I finally figured out what these people had in common. They all walked their talk all day, every day. They didn't just celebrate the sabbats; they *lived* their Witchcraft beliefs in every facet of their lives—not in big, bold "look at me, I'm a Witch" statements (which is probably why it took me so long to put my finger on just what it was I was looking at) but in quiet, subtle ways that touched on who and what they were at a core level.

These folks had succeeded in finding ways to integrate their spiritual beliefs into their everyday lives, walking their paths 24/7 in small and large ways. Once I realized that, I knew that *this* was the kind of Witch I wanted to be. It was the birth of major shift in my own personal path, as well as the inspiration for both *The Goddess Is in the Details* and the book you hold in your hands right now.

While it may sound like becoming one of these "everyday Witches" is impossible, in fact, it is fairly simple. You just have to decide that this is the path for you and then put your foot on the first step and then the next and the next.

As a bonus, I thought it might be fun to read about the different paths a few other folks have chosen to follow. Each is very different but is the right road for the one who chose it. Throughout this book, I've asked some other Pagan authors to share their stories with you—for fun, for inspiration, and to cast some light on the many different approaches that can all lead to the place we most want to be: at home in our own personal practice.

Some of them have different points of view or suggestions for ways to practice that I never would have thought of. I couldn't ask for better voices than the lovely authors who very kindly added their contributions to mine.

The Benefits of Religious Pluralism
BLAKE OCTAVIAN BLAIR

Modern Paganism is full of potential, growth, and autonomy, which is what attracted many of us to start down this path. I have always felt that there isn't one true way but rather many valid pathways to the truth. My personal practice of Paganism has always been rooted in respect and celebration of this viewpoint.

I began my path practicing a fairly generic brand of modern Witchcraft and Paganism. It was rather utilitarian. It allowed me to express my desire for and practice of earth-centered spirituality while letting me explore and learn about various more specific Pagan paths and the theologies, rituals, and practices that accompany them, and explore the many manifestations of the Divine that exist among world religions. Pagans in general tend to have a love for the study and exploration of world religions; for me, it led to minoring in religion during my university studies.

I have always attempted to go about the act of spiritual exploration with an open heart and open mind. With this approach, instead of looking for what elements were a fit for me and resonated with my path, those elements began to make themselves known to me! Deities began to visit me and leave signs of their presence and guidance. I often find when dealing with divine forces that those with whom we're meant to work will find us; we need not search in desperation for them as long as we keep our senses open to their presence and messages. Such encounters and messages are how I came to work with the Hindu pantheon and learned to integrate traditional elements of *puja* (ritual worship) as part of my personal path.

My viewpoint of deity has always been of the polytheistic variety. I feel this has greatly contributed to my open-mindedness and ease of accepting viewpoints that are less familiar to me and perhaps differ from my own. I don't feel a need for any type of mandated "either/or" theology; I've always theologically swayed much more toward allowing for the possibility of a "both/and" paradigm. I do not believe that the existence of one particular view of God, divinity, or the afterlife must preclude another. Having this open viewpoint can lead one into learning experiences, interactions, and exposure to and with many new and different perspectives that can shape and lead to revision of one's personal views.

My path has continued to grow and evolve to include my training to become a Reiki Master-Teacher and shamanic practitioner. I continue to practice magick and spellcraft and honor the Hindu pantheon within my practice. However, I would currently define my path as primarily a shamanic one that includes an animistic viewpoint and engages heavily with the natural and spirit world.

A spiritual path is a living thing, and living things grow and change. Many people fear change when it involves their spiritual practice or theology for various reasons. However, growth involves change. If we do not grow, we risk begrudgingly plodding down a path that doesn't serve our highest good. We must allow ourselves to expand, revise, and find our own spiritual truth and path. A healthy spiritual path is one that includes constant growth. Growth almost inherently includes change. I wish you many blessings as you forge the path that lies ahead!

Creating Your Personal Path
CHRISTOPHER PENCZAK

We are always creating our own personal path. Even when you are following a particular tradition, you are walking your own way and in your own time upon the path. What brought you to that tradition and what keeps you there is different for every practitioner, so, in essence, we all create our own way, looking for teachers, elders, books, and communities to help us along the way. One of my favorite spiritual ancestors is the occultist Dion Fortune, author of many books including *The Sea Priestess*, who wrote "the ways to God are as many as the breaths of the sons of men" (*Esoteric Orders and Their Work*, chapter 13). While she was working in a Christian magick framework, it essentially means that for every person, there is a way to the Divine.

One of the difficulties in modern spirituality—in truly and consciously walking our own path—is the tendency to grab the things we like and discard the things that don't appeal to us but that ultimately might be more important to us. People describe it as the "salad bar" mentality of spirituality. Just like little kids, we don't eat our vegetables. While there is wisdom in finding the material that resonates with us, we sometimes think *resonate* means "things we like"—and really it means "causes a vibration or a reaction within us." If we don't like something, we should investigate it to see if we are missing out on something important. The things that are unimportant won't carry any charge for us, for good or ill, but the things we love and the things we hate and fear are our greatest teachers in walking the path.

When crafting practices for your personal path, look to some traditional magickal patterns to make sure you are working with a complete picture. That way you won't avoid the necessary but sometimes less than pleasant aspects of any path. Despite the popular misconceptions, the world is not always love and light. In traditional Wicca, there is a saying that one must be prepared to suffer in order to learn. Not all learning is suffering, but we learn from all experiences.

By magickal pattern, I mean a way the magick is divided, categorized, and experienced that is in the entire spectrum of experience. The elements—earth, air, fire, and water—are a complete pattern, particularly if you include the fifth element of spirit. They embody the principles of the body, mind, soul, and emotions, along with the interconnecting principle of spirit. The archetypes found in the seven planets are another complete system, even without the "modern" planets. In it we have the sun and moon deities along with the messengers: the love god, the war god, the sky god, and the lord of karma and consequences.

The shaman's model has three simple worlds that are complete as a model, with a realm above dealing with the lofty and seen principles, the realm below comprising the unconscious and unseen, and the world between in the center connecting the two through nature, seasons, time, and space. Add the four directions as the four elements and you have an even more complete seven-point system.

Let those who have come before you guide you in the process of your own path. Their wisdom has survived because it has worked, and you honor their lives by putting it to good use here and now.

The Everyday Witch

I like to call myself the everyday Witch, and you'll see that reflected in a number of my book titles, like *Everyday Witch Book of Rituals* or *Everyday Witch A to Z Spellbook*. Even *The Goddess Is in the Details* is subtitled *Wisdom for the Everyday Witch*.

So what does that mean, the everyday Witch?

Two things, really.

For one thing, I'm just an everyday Witch—nothing fancy or special. I don't lead a major coven, and I haven't started my own Witchcraft movement that has grown to encompass many, such as Christopher Penczak or Raymond Buckland or Z Budapest have. (All folks I admire and respect, but I'm so not in that class; I'm not a professional Witch who teaches thousands and is known all over the world. I'm just little ol' me.)

I lead a predominantly average life. A tad unconventional compared to some, maybe, since I'm a writer and craftsperson and run a shop full of artists, all of which allow me to be more open about my witchy leanings than some people might be able to. But still, I am like most other people: I work, I take care of my little farmhouse in the country, and I get bossed around by cats on a daily basis.

A few people might know me from my books, but, for the most part, I'm just an everyday Witch. Much like almost any other Witch you might meet, I'm a woman trying to juggle the responsibilities and obligations of daily life while at the same time attempting to better myself and be the best "me" I can be.

The other meaning of the term "everyday Witch" has to do with my commitment to walking my talk every day. I like to think that I am a Witch all day, every day, instead of just during the time of the full moons or during the eight sabbats. This is usually reflected in small things, not large ones. I do a bit of kitchen alchemy in the morning when I make my breakfast hot chocolate, mixing mundane ingredients with magickal intentions. I greet the gods briefly when I wake up and thank them before I fall asleep. I try to live as green a life as possible because, to me, taking care of the earth is part of being a Witch, too.

Nothing big or complicated, as you can see; just integrating my beliefs into my regular life—an everyday Witch.

Most of the Witches I talk to would like to be everyday Witches, too. Not everyone, of course—plenty of folks are perfectly happy to only focus on their spiritual nature eight or thirteen or so times a year, and that's just fine. As long as that's the kind of practice that suits them, I think that's great.

But for many, it isn't that they don't *want* to be everyday Witches, it's more a matter of *how*. They don't know how to find the time and space and energy in the midst of their busy lives, or they can't figure out how to integrate their spiritual path with the rest of their world without having to chase down exotic ingredients, go through complicated and drawn-out rituals, or explain to the neighbors why they're dancing naked on the lawn. (Kidding about that last one. Mostly.)

This book is written by me, an everyday Witch, for all those who would also like to be everyday Witches. Just people who live their lives and happen to be Pagan. The naked dancing is optional.

Daily Practice

Many spiritual paths include some form of daily practice. Buddhism, for instance, encourages meditation as well as a general attitude of mindfulness. Some religions focus more on daily prayer or saying grace before each meal as a way of giving thanks. Some have prayer beads or rosaries. Devout Muslims kneel in prayer multiple times a day.

But these practices tend to be limited to the most devoted followers, and not everyone follows them. Traditionally, modern Witchcraft hasn't really had any guidelines for daily practice, and people often have trouble coming up with something on their own.

I'd been trying for years to integrate some form of daily practice into my spiritual path when I came across a wonderful book called *The Circle Within: Creating a Wiccan Spiritual Tradition* by Dianne Sylvan. The author advocated a commonsense approach to finding the daily practice that was right for you, and reading her book made me take a new look at what I'd been doing.

Mostly, my mistake had been of the "square peg, round hole" variety. I'd come up with all sorts of complicated or time-consuming daily practices when what I really needed was something quick and easy.

Now I have a few daily practices, all of which help me connect with deity and my own Witchcraft path, and none of which take more than a few minutes to perform.

In the morning, before I even get out of bed (often before I open my eyes), I greet the gods and ask them for their assistance through the course of my day. Here's what I usually say (and if you want to use this as part of your daily practice, substitute whatever words work for you):

> *God and Goddess, I greet you at the start of another day and ask that*
> *you send me the best day possible. Help me to feel my best so I might do*
> *my best for myself and for others. Send me the strength and energy to*
> *do the things I need to do, and the focus and creativity to do them well.*
> *Help me to let go of all those things that no longer work for my benefit*
> *so I might move in the direction of perfect health and perfect balance.*

Please send me prosperity and healing, patience and wisdom, serenity and faith.* Guide me as I walk the path of the author; help me to write rapidly, easily, and well, and let my words please those who read them. Keep my cats healthy and safe, help the world move in a better direction, and watch over me and those I love. So mote it be.

*The things I ask for vary from day to day, depending on what is going on in my life. For instance, if I have an important event, I might ask for it to go well. If I am going to get some sort of healing work done, like visiting the acupuncturist or chiropractor, I might ask for the work to be helpful and long lasting. Obviously, you would tailor this to whatever works best for you.

After I have turned off the light at night, I always say thank you to the gods for my day. There are some things I always thank them for, and then I add the people and events that have been particularly important that day. I often give thanks for stuff that might seem unpleasant or negative if I feel as though I have learned something from it or if I think something good might come from it down the road. (For instance, when someone rear-ended my brand-new car, I gave thanks that the damage was minimal, no one was hurt, and that the first boo-boo was out of the way without it being my fault!)

Remember that you can change the words to suit your own needs, and that there are always different things to give thanks for. The important part of doing this as a part of your daily ritual is that not only does it show the gods that you are taking an attitude of gratitude (always a good thing, in my opinion), but it also forces you to find *something* about your day to be grateful for, no matter how small it is. I am always surprised to find that there is more to say thank you for than I would have expected. Here is an example of what I might say last thing at night:

Great Goddess, Great God, I come before you at the end of another day and thank you for the many blessings in my life. For friends and family and cats, for home and health and good food. I thank

you for (the names of whichever people crossed my path that day
in meaningful ways) and for (whatever good things happened or
whichever not-so-great things they helped me survive). Please help me
to get a good night's sleep so I might wake in the morning refreshed
and energized and ready to face another day. Watch over me and those
I love. So mote it be.

There are a few other things that I try to do daily, including meditation, some form of mindful exercise, and lighting a candle and saying a spell or a prayer. I don't always manage it, though. What I *do* always manage is to find a minute to appreciate nature, whether it is a beautiful sunrise, the mist rising off the meadow next to my house, the song of the birds outside my window, or the sound of the rain. Those things only take a moment, and they lift my heart every time. These, too, are ways to practice Witchcraft, since we are a nature-based religion.

Here are some suggestions for easy, fast ways to integrate a daily practice into your life. Choose the ones that work best for you, and create your own personal daily rituals.

Start the Day

You don't have to use my approach to starting the day; there are plenty of other ways to begin a new day with a spiritual touch.

- Greet the Goddess and/or God in your own way. Or say:
  Lord and Lady, I greet thee. Bless my path on this new day,
  and watch over me as I walk it to the best of my ability.

- Greet the dawn or the new sun. Use your own words or say:
  I greet you, new day! I greet the dawn! I greet the sun!
  I greet the earth below and the sky above! Blessings upon the day!

- Light a candle each morning on an altar. (If you will be leaving the house to go to work, you might want to light the candle, say something, then snuff it out right away so you don't have to worry about forgetting it.) You can say whatever words are in your heart that morning or use one of the greetings above. Or you can say this:

With this light, I greet the new day.

(See? It doesn't have to be any more complicated than that.)

- Ask the gods or the universe for help with any issues you might be having. You can say something like this:

  At the start of this new day, I ask for help with _____ and vow to do my very best with what I am given.

- Take a moment of silence to listen to the world around you before diving into the noise and bustle of the day. Listen to the sounds inside your home: maybe people or animals stirring, maybe just the ticking of a clock…maybe nothing at all, which is a gift in and of itself. Listen to the sounds from outside: birds, the wind, rain, the sound of traffic or people going by. Feel the connection you have with the rest of the world, and give yourself that moment to be quiet before diving into your busy day. If you want, say a few words to the gods—they can hear you even when you don't speak out loud. (This is an especially good daily routine for those who can't practice openly.)

- Read an affirmation or an inspiring passage, either from a book or from something you have written down ahead of time. (Multiple lists of books can be found at the end of this book, or use your own favorites.)

- Write in a journal. Taking a few moments to be present with your own thoughts, and writing down your hopes and dreams, can be a helpful part of a spiritual journey.

- Take a walk outside and commune with nature. There is nothing like connecting with the gods and the world outside by taking a morning walk, especially if you are lucky enough to have someplace quiet and peaceful to do so, like a park or a country road. Maybe leave the music at home and simply listen to the sounds around you. As a bonus, you get exercise, too!

To me, one of the most important components of a Pagan path is connection: connection with the gods, with nature, with each other, with our own inner voices. If you can start your day off by making that connection, it is like giving a gift to your spiritual self!

End the Day

- Thank the Goddess, the God, or the universe in general for another day. You can use the previous words, say whatever comes to mind, or you can say:

  Lord and Lady, I bid you good night. I thank you for the blessings of the day and for all the gifts you bring to my life. Grant me a peaceful night and a bright tomorrow. Blessed be.

- Watch the sunset. Walk outside and look at the moon, if you can see her, and blow a kiss to the Lady above. Make a wish on a star.

- Take a shower to wash away the negative energy of the day (being mindful of that goal as opposed to just taking a shower to get clean) or waft a sage wand over yourself.

- Say a nightly prayer. This is especially nice for those who grew up with the tradition of a nightly prayer but no longer wish to use the words from their childhood. Say whatever is in your heart, or you can use this:

  Bless me, Goddess, as I bid goodbye to another day. Bless my home and my family, bless this planet on which I live, and bless me with your infinite love and grace.

Light a Candle

- You can do this at a set time every day or whenever you can squeeze it in. If you have an altar, you may wish to light your candle there, but it is fine to put your candle wherever it will be safe and out of the way. You can say a small prayer or blessing, or simply take a moment to close your eyes and feel gratitude. Alternately, you can gaze at the light and see it as a symbol for the light your spiritual path brings to your life.

- If you want, you can light four candles—one each for earth, air, fire, and water—or two candles, one for the Goddess and one for the God.

- Any candle will do, but if you want to add an extra magickal element to this act, you can anoint the candle with some kind of magickal oil or use a special candle you have blessed and consecrated ahead of time. You can also carve runes or symbols into the candle to symbolize healing, prosperity, love, or whatever else you might want to bring into your life.

- If you prefer, you can light incense or burn some sage instead. Either way, if you are using something with a smell to it, use the odor to remind you that you are taking a sacred moment.

Say a Prayer or a Spell

- Say the same prayer or spell every day at the same time. Repetition can help to put you into that "sacred space" kind of feeling, even if it is just for a few minutes.

- Say whatever prayer or spell seems to be most suitable for that particular day. For instance, if you are having a tough time at work or with the people you share your life with, you can say a prayer or spell for patience (or energy or whatever else you need that day).

- Write a daily spell or prayer and place it on your altar or somewhere you will be sure to see it (even the fridge or the bathroom mirror) so you won't forget to say it when things get hectic.

- Here is an example of a simple prayer you can use:

God and Goddess, hear my daily prayer
Grant me patience and serenity as I walk through your world
Shelter me and those I love from harm
Light my way as I walk my path
And hold me in your loving arms
So mote it be

Connect with Nature

Witchcraft is a nature-based religion, but many of us don't spend much time communing with nature—we're too busy rushing from place to place trying to get everything done. Try taking a few minutes every day to make that connection in a mindful way. It doesn't have to take long, and you don't need to make a special trip to the ocean or the mountains (although that's a good idea every once in a while). Here are a few easy options:

- Open a window. What can you hear or smell or see that belongs to the natural world?

- Listen to the birds or the rain or a thunderstorm.

- Take a walk (yes, even if it is raining).

- Take off your shoes and walk on the grass or put your feet into the dirt.

- Connect with water—ocean or stream, pond or puddle.

- Connect with air—feel the wind on your face, smell the flowers on the breeze, blow a few bubbles.

- Connect with fire—light a bonfire outside and enjoy the smells and sounds of the crackling flames.

- Connect with earth—dig in the dirt, plant something, sit on the ground and feel the energy of the earth beneath you.

- Talk a walk in a forest or a park. Hug a tree!

- Play in the leaves in the fall.

- Play in the snow in the winter. You're never too old to make a snow angel or build a snowman or snow goddess.

- Go outside at night and look up at the sky. Can you see the moon? The stars? A planet? (Venus is often visible to the naked eye.) Find a book on constellations and become familiar with a few.

Meditate

Meditation isn't hard or complicated. Like anything else you do, it gets easier with practice, but don't worry if you can't make your mind stop racing around in circles or if you can't twist yourself into a pretzel to sit in the "proper" position. Essentially, meditation is just taking a few moments to be quiet—to stop moving and sit in one place, to give yourself the space to connect with your inner voice, with the rhythms of your body, with the gods. You can give yourself five or ten minutes a day, can't you? Of course you can.

- The simplest form of meditation is just this: sit in a comfortable position (or lie down, if you won't fall asleep) and breathe. Turn off the phone and the TV. Close your eyes, and breathe slowly and deeply. Pay attention to your breath as it comes in and goes out. If you want, you can say a word in your head with each inhalation (such as "calm" or "peace") and a word with each exhalation (such as "release" or "love"). Or you can simply breathe, and allow yourself to be at peace with the universe.

- If you want to get slightly more involved, you can add in visualization. When I meditate, I see myself surrounded by a bubble of protective light filled with loving, healing energy. As I breathe, I take in that energy and breathe out the tension and stress of the day. I also sometimes visualize myself connecting with the energy of the sky above (through my crown chakra) and the ground below (through my root chakra).

- Try opening yourself to the God or Goddess during meditation. Close your eyes and feel the love of the gods surrounding you, encompassing you in warmth and acceptance.

- You can also add a magickal component to your meditation practice. I usually start by doing tai chi for about ten minutes, then placing a table in front of the spot where I meditate. I sit on my meditation cushion, light a candle, and talk to the gods; then I say a spell. After that, I close my eyes and begin my meditation. These three things work surprisingly well together, and I am accomplishing three of my daily practices in the same twenty to thirty minutes (or less, if it is a busy day).

Repeat an Affirmation

An affirmation is basically a positive statement either said silently or out loud. You can stand in front of a mirror and say it, incorporate it into your meditation, or say it in bed when you wake up or right before you go to sleep (or any other time that feels right to you).

Affirmations are always said in the present tense ("I am strong and healthy" as opposed to "I will be strong and healthy"), as if they were already true—even if they are something you are still working at bringing to fruition. They are often repeated a number of times. They are believed to work by convincing your subconscious (or maybe the universe) that what you have repeated so many times must be true.

Affirmations are said for yourself and should reflect your own needs and desires. They don't have to stay the same.

Here are a few possible affirmations. You can come up with your own, too.

- The gods love me, and so I love myself.

- I open myself to all the good things the universe has to offer.

- I am strong and healthy. My body is balanced and working perfectly.

- My life is filled with joy and fulfillment.

- I am the stuff that stars are made of. I am divine. I am Goddess/
  God.

Say Thank You for Your Food

Many religions have a tradition of giving thanks for the food we eat, but
in this modern age, few people stop to say grace or consider where our food
comes from or what it goes through to get from farms and fields to our
plates. Partially, this is due to a disconnect between farm and table; most
people never see meat that doesn't come wrapped in plastic from a grocery
store case, few shop at farmers' markets and meet the people who grow
their lettuce or apples, and even fewer grow their own food.

And that's fine if you don't have access to a garden or freshly grown
local produce. But it is still a good idea to take a moment before eating to
give thanks to the people who grew, harvested, and transported your food,
as well as send out appreciation to any animals involved. (Some people
choose not to eat meat at all, and that is another issue, but if you are going
to eat meat, the least you can do is be grateful for the sacrifice of the animal
involved.)

I don't say a formal grace before eating (it wasn't one of the traditions I
grew up with), but I do raise my glass or mug in a silent toast to the Goddess and God and to all those who produced my food. I also take a moment
to be grateful that I have enough to eat and that I have food I like when so
many are hungry or eating substandard fare just to survive.

If you want something a little more substantial than that, you can say
something like this:

> God and Goddess, bless this food that it may nourish my body and my
> spirit. I give thanks for the food and for all who contributed to producing
> it. So mote it be.

Mindful Exercise

You might be thinking, "What does exercise have to do with a spiritual practice?" It depends on the exercise, of course, but we all know that there is no real separation between mind, body, and spirit. And if you choose to do a form of exercise that nurtures these things together, it can definitely become part of a spiritual practice.

There are a few types of exercise that lend themselves particularly well to being done in a mindful way and in a calm, quiet space where you can open your spirit as you move your body. A few to try include:

- yoga

- tai chi

- chi gong

- belly dance

- walking (some people do walking meditation instead of sitting meditation, or you can chant quietly to yourself as you walk, channeling God/dess like a walking prayer)

- swimming (if you are someplace quiet, not in a public pool)

Read a Book

I'm not talking about a murder mystery, of course. But there are many great books that can be used as part of a daily spiritual practice. Some Christians read the Bible every day to keep themselves connected to their religion. And while there is no such thing as a Pagan bible, there are plenty of books that can be sources of inspiration; some of my favorites are listed in chapter 11.

You can pick a book and read one section every day (this works especially well if you are using a "365" book that has something for each day of the year). You can also have a few books and pick whichever one you are in the mood for.

I like to do my spiritual reading at night when I'm in bed, right before I go to sleep, but I have a friend who prefers to do hers in the quiet of the morning. She says that little bit of inspiration with her morning tea gets her day off to a good start. She likes to read various poets, too, since poetry can be inspirational and uplifting.

Prayer Beads

You can buy or make a string of beads that you use, much as Christians use a rosary, to help you say a repetitive form of prayer. You can find instructions for making them on the Internet. If you grew up Catholic and later became a Pagan and miss having a rosary, this can be a nice compromise. (Buddhists use prayer beads too, as do some other religions.)

There are plenty of other ways to integrate a daily practice into your life. Choose something that appeals to you—that you will actually *want* to do every day. And don't be discouraged if your daily practice doesn't happen every single day. Try to pick things that will be doable given your own particular schedule, obligations, and inclinations, and then just do your best.

Connecting with Deity

One of the main reasons why none of the spiritual paths I tried when I was younger worked out for me was because I was never able to make a connection with deity through any of them.

In fact, if you had asked me then, I would probably have told you that I was an agnostic—I believed it was possible that some form of god existed, but I had never experienced anything personally that would have proven it to me.

That all changed the night I took part in my first ritual, gathered into a circle with a bunch of people I didn't know. It was dark, I was a little uncomfortable, and I didn't really expect very much.

And yet, from the first moment the circle was cast, I felt *something*—something I had never felt before: call it magick, call it connection. Suddenly I could *feel* the presence of the God and Goddess around me and within me. It was a revelation and a gift. It was also the start of the Pagan path I still walk today.

It has always seemed to me that the gods and goddesses of modern Witchcraft are more accessible than the often stern and far-removed God of the Judeo-Christian religions. In truth, I suspect that deity comes to each of us in whichever form we can most readily connect with; sometimes it simply takes more searching to find the form that is most suited to your needs.

Either way, just as with communication with other human beings, communication with deity takes some effort and a willingness to be open to that connection. For many of us, being able to have that relationship with whichever god, goddess, or gods we worship is a core element of our practice, but it's also something that often gets lost in our daily lives.

Here are a few simple, easy ways to work on that connection:

Have a Chat

Pagan gods don't usually require the formal, ornate approach that some other deities do. While there is nothing wrong with a long, complicated ritual (if you have the time and inclination for one), communicating with deity can be as simple as talking a walk in the woods or sitting in your own living room and saying, "You know, there is something I'd like to talk to you about…"

There is no need to have a priest or a church; all Witches are priests and priestesses in their own right and can speak to God/dess directly. For some of the folks I know who consider themselves Pagans (as opposed to Witches or Wiccans), the forests and the fields are as close to a temple as they get, and an informal chat is the only ritual they need. So if you don't have time to cast a circle or light candles for a formal invocation, you can still connect with deity.

Say a Prayer

If you want to move things a step up from a chat, you can say a prayer. Prayer is simply another form, usually a little more formal, of talking to the gods. You may start by saying something to call the God/ddess' attention to you, such as, "Great God, great Goddess, please hear my prayer." Or you can light a candle while standing at your altar, if you have one. Prayer is usually a way to ask for help, whether it is with something general ("please send me patience") or something specific ("help me to do well on this test").

Spells can be a form of prayer and are also a kind of communication with deity.

Invoke the God/Goddess During Ritual

You can, of course, call on the gods formally during ritual. The Goddess and God are usually invoked during spellcasting and ritual work, often by lighting a candle and saying something like, "Lady of the Moon, we ask that you join us in our sacred rite held in your honor." Solitary rituals offer a chance for more personal communication, although that can happen during group rituals as well, depending on the circumstances. If you recall, my first connection with deity was made during a formal (and quite large) ritual, and yet I very clearly felt their attention focus on me in that moment.

Put Up an Altar

For an ongoing connection to the God, Goddess, or deities of your choice, it is nice to have an altar dedicated to him/her/them or use a specific image of that deity on your regular altar. Not everyone has a specific god or goddess they follow. My friend Lisa is dedicated to Yemaya and has a number of statues in her image. I, on the other hand, tend to talk to a non-specific god and goddess, and so whatever figures I use on my altars (I have three) are usually also fairly general—a horned god and a female figure, for instance.

Put Up a Picture, Statue, or Image

You don't have to have an altar in order to honor deity, nor do you need to limit yourself to that space. Lots of people put up Pagan images of gods and goddesses or of statues that resemble the primitive figures used by ancient Pagans.

Drawing Down the Moon

One very specific way to commune with the Goddess is a rite known as "drawing down the moon." This is done on the night of the full moon, usually by a high priestess, but it can also be done by anyone. It is a way of literally inviting the Goddess to enter the body and spirit of the person calling her down and allowing the Goddess to speak through that person. There is a poem called "The Charge of the Goddess" that is often recited (it is long and beautiful, and usually memorized for the occasion), although some people simply open themselves to the power of the Goddess by standing under the full moon and sending out a mental call. Either way, channeling the Goddess is a powerful experience that is not to be done lightly. I don't recommend it for beginners, but only you can judge when you are ready to attempt it.

Read a Book

One of the best ways to make a connection to deity is by finding out more about her or him. If you have a particular goddess or god that you feel is calling to you, by all means, do some research and find out all you can. If you aren't sure whether there is one god or another who is "the" deity for you, that is all the more reason to explore. Or you can find a few books that will aid you in making a connection with deity, with or without a specific name.

(There are a few of my personal favorites listed at the end of this book. You can find many more online, I'm sure, as well as resources.)

Listen

Lastly, more than any of the options I've mentioned above, there is this: LISTEN.

You can say all the prayers and spells you want, but if you do not make a space of silence in which to listen to the answers, it is all for nothing. If there is one thing I have learned in all my years as a practicing Witch, it is that the gods are very willing to speak to us; the problem often lies in our willingness to listen to them.

So my advice, for whatever it is worth, is to take a few moments a day to wait, to listen, and to hear. You never know who will be speaking to you if you are willing to listen.

Bringing Magick into Your Everyday Life

Regular life is filled with the mundane. We have to clean our homes, go to work, make food, pay bills… Often there seems to be little room for the magickal in the midst of all the necessary chores that make up our everyday lives.

But, in fact, all these things are opportunities for magick.

Remember that for most Pagans in days gone by, there was no separation between the mundane and the magickal. Protection spells were spun into yarn; healing herbs were tucked into sachets under pillows and tossed into soups and stews. Witches hid their magick in plain sight by using it to cook and sew and sweep with. As modern Witches, we can do the same—hidden or not—by integrating our magickal work with the tasks we do every day.

What follows are a few examples of ways to do this. If they don't suit you, all you have to do is look at your daily life, break it down into tasks, and figure out ways to make a few of them magickal.

Food Magick

Putting a magickal touch into the food you prepare—whether for yourself or for those you love—is a tried and true Witchcraft tradition. I'm not talking about sneaking a love potion into someone's drink (never a good idea, believe me). But women and men have been stirring magick into their food since the dawn of time. Spices to warm the heart, herbs for protection and health—all these things have been used for centuries, and there is no reason why you can't come up with your own modern variations on the theme.

For instance, I mentioned before that I do what I call "kitchen alchemy" every morning when I make my hot chocolate. You're probably wondering how hot chocolate could be magickal (well, other than the chocolate part, which is pretty wonderful all by itself). As with most magick, it has to do with focus and intent.

Because I make it so often, I actually have a nifty machine that mixes, heats, and froths the hot chocolate. As I place each ingredient inside, I focus on its magickal qualities: milk for health and healing; chocolate for prosperity and love; a spoonful of honey for healing and energy; a pinch of cayenne pepper for energy and creativity; a bit of cinnamon for prosperity and love; and coffee for energy. (Yes, technically, this makes it mocha.)

It is just that easy. Take a food or drink that you already make, and find its magickal qualities. Almost all foods have some, and how you use them is only limited by your imagination. For instance, if you are having a special dinner with your significant other, you can use ingredients that enhance love, such as apples, cinnamon, and chocolate. Dessert, anyone? You can't make someone love you with magickal food, but you can use it to help create a positive mood.

If you are packing a lunch for a child, why not add in some protective or love foods and herbs? Spread a little mustard on a sandwich and visualize its protection qualities. A handful of almonds is good for both health and protection. Having the boss over for dinner? Throw some herbs for success into the stew. (Okay—don't make a stew if your boss is coming over. That's just wrong. But you see my point.)

Fiber and Clothing Magick

People—women especially—have been using fiber for magickal work forever. Back in the days when people made their own clothing, it was easy to spin protection into the wool your husband wore while he was out hunting or put love into every stitch of a quilt. But you don't have to spin or weave to use fiber magick, and now, as then, your endeavors can be subtle and hidden from sight.

Here are a few suggestions for ways to use thread, yarn, and clothing to work everyday magick with no one the wiser.

KNOT MAGICK—Knots are a traditional form of binding magick, which ties your intentions into string, ribbon, or whatever you are knotting. You can make a knotted bracelet out of colorful fibers and reinforce your goal (healing, prosperity, etc.) with every knot you tie. You can also do knot magick while you are sewing. For instance, if you have a child going off to camp and you are sewing name labels into her clothing, simply tie extra knots and fill each one with your wish for protection. For a fast and easy magickal spell, use any piece of string or yarn and say the following while tying nine knots and visualizing your desire:

By the knot of one, the spell's begun
By the knot of two, it cometh true
By the knot of three, so mote it be
By the knot of four, open the door
By the knot of five, the spell's alive
By the knot of six, the spell is fixed
By the knot of seven, the stars of heaven
By the knot of eight, the stroke of fate
By the knot of nine, this thing is mine!

THREAD MAGICK—It is also easy to work magick with nothing more than a simple needle and thread. Just use the thread to sew a symbol or rune into a piece of clothing, like a heart on the inside of a shirt or jacket for someone whom you want to feel your love all day, or the rune Gifu (which looks like an X) for prosperity on the inside of your purse or wallet.

CLOTHING MAGICK—Clothing itself can be used to put an intention out into the universe. One of Blue Moon Circle's former members always chose the color of her underwear depending on what kind of energy she needed from that particular day: green for prosperity, black for protection, red for energy, orange for courage, and so on. I tend to do the same with my clothing in general. I usually wear a bit of green or brown on Thursdays, since that's the day for prosperity work, and I put on my prosperity necklace, too.

KNITTING, CROCHETING, SPINNING, WEAVING, QUILTING, SEWING—If you are fortunate enough to have some talent in any of these areas, you can integrate magick as you do your craft; it is as simple as focusing on the essence you want to go into your finished project with every movement. I don't do any fiber crafts, but when I make jewelry I often imbue a special piece with love and energy for whatever I think the person needs the most.

Musical Magick

Music is a powerful tool. It can evoke emotion, soothe the spirit, raise energy, and even be used to commune with the gods. It is also easy to carry with you in the form of your own voice. There are many ways to integrate a Pagan element into your music and bring that into your everyday life. Here are just a few examples:

SING IN THE SHOWER—No, there is nothing particularly magickal about singing in the shower—unless you are using a nice witchy chant. Then you can start or end your day on an uplifting spiritual note. My particular favorites are the classic "She Changes Everything She Touches" or "Fire Am I," but there are lots of great ones out there. Check out YouTube or find a CD with chants on it if you don't already have ones you use.

PLAY A WITCHY CD—I like to play music while I am cleaning the house or exercising, as well as when I'm driving in my car. Sometimes I use it as the backdrop to my meditation or ritual work, too. There are lots of amazing Pagan musicians, like Wendy Rule and Gabrielle Roth. I am also partial to Heather Alexander, Troika (try their *Goddess* CD), and a British group called Daughters of Gaia (they do a great rock-and-roll CD called *Rock the Goddess* with modern updates of some traditional chants, as well as some that they wrote themselves). No matter what kind of witchy music you choose to listen to, it is an easy way to bring a Pagan flavor to your regular daily activities.

DRUM—Pagans have been drumming since the dawn of time, as far as anyone can tell. Drums can be reasonably inexpensive, and they aren't necessarily an obviously Pagan tool (lots of people have drums, after all, and they aren't all Witches by any means). Once or twice a week you can set aside a few minutes to drum, connecting with the heartbeat of the earth. Drumming's rhythmic beat can be relaxing and meditative, even inducing trances for spiritual traveling. Or it can be invigorating and uplifting after a long, tough day. People from all over the world have used the sound of drums to communicate with their gods, and you can, too. If you don't have a drum or the inclination to do the drumming yourself, there are plenty of good drum CDs out there. There are ones that are particularly witchy or Native American or New Age in general. Just find one that you like and put it on as you exercise or meditate, or you can pull out your own drum and play along.

There are lots of other fast and easy ways to bring magick into your everyday life. I'll be talking about integrating magickal work with housecleaning later in the book, as well as a few other approaches. Just keep in mind that you can always find something that fits your own particular lifestyle and needs; you just have to be willing to try!

Witchcraft and Personal Empowerment
RAVEN DIGITALIS

Many people get attracted to Neopaganism and Witchcraft because it gives them a sense of empowerment in life's craziness. Others enter the Craft for a sense of power, which is quite different from empowerment, and sometimes with the goal of achieving control over other people or situations. Empowerment, however, is more akin to self-mastery and self-awareness, and it's from this springboard that new Witches can jump from a "let's do some spells" mentality to a "let's live our Craft" frame of mind.

Modern Witches are influenced by Wicca (even if they don't want to admit it), which was, in turn, influenced by Celtic Paganism, old-world folk charmery, the Hermetic Golden Dawn, Freemasonry, grimoire systems of Western ceremonial magick, and so on. Magickal traditions are inherently incestuous, and there's nothing wrong with it!

Wicca was created without any real moral edicts or regulations, aside from the famed line in the Wiccan Rede: An' it harm none, do what ye will. This line, first presented by Doreen Valiente (Gerald Gardner's high priestess) is actually most likely influenced by Aleister Crowley's esoteric system of Thelema. Thelema is Greek for "will," and in this case will refers to a person's true spiritual destiny—a person's higher course in life that occurs every second of every minute. I would say that this is the true meaning of that particular verse of the Rede—more of a "do what you're meant to be doing" rather than "do whatever you want."

I would argue that a person's will necessarily includes community service, public assistance, or other forms of helping others—another person, animals, the ecosystem, and so on—have a better quality of life. It's good for us Pagans to consider the bigger picture on a regular basis. What are we here to do? Are we making progressive decisions? Are we helping others or mainly ourselves? Are we living with kindness and using our magick in ways that will have lasting positive effects?

So, how are you making a difference on a daily basis? The possibilities are limitless. Recycling everything possible is a daily practice that helps the earth and can lessen our carbon footprint. Volunteer work and community service are common fields for spiritual people who want to make a difference. Some people work in animal shelters or homeless shelters, or are regular activists for human rights or animal rights. Some people make significant art. Others humbly pursue paths of teaching and leadership.

The manner in which we regularly interact with other people is key. It's easy to get caught in the human trappings of ego. It's valiant to set aside our pride so we can explore empathy with even the most difficult individuals.

If we truly have a desire to love our lives rather than fight every step of the way, everything falls into place. If we control our own actions and strive for positive responses, life has a way of giving us more pleasant experiences and interactions. Actions and emotions tend to have ripple effects.

It's also essential to consider where we are putting our money. Are we supporting the local economy or are we feeding the corporate greed monster? Are we consuming local produce and humanely raised animals or are we encouraging the evils of factory "farming" or the earth-killing, large-scale "agriculture" machine?

To help increase self-awareness, it may also be a good idea to form a daily practice that may include positive visualizations, breathing exercises, yoga, protection rituals, affirmations, meditation, chants, and so on. By creating daily practices, a practitioner can feel more grounded and centered in reality, allowing for more mindful choices to be made on a daily basis. By consciously consuming and by choosing love-based human interactions, our empathy increases and so does our engagement in this strange thing called life. By bettering ourselves, we better the world, creating a solid path of living magick.

Making Time for Spirit in a Too-Busy World

If there is one thing that most of us have in common, it is this: we are BUSY, BUSY people leading BUSY, BUSY lives.

I don't know anyone who isn't over-maxed. Between work and family and pets and home and pets (sorry, Magic the Cat made me put that one in twice) and the myriad things that occupy our time, most of us have a hard time finding enough hours to eat and sleep, much less carve out space for spirit in our day-to-day lives. Surely it is enough to be *theoretically* Pagan, perhaps going to a sabbat celebration or paying attention to the full moon once in a while.

If you thought that was true, you probably wouldn't be reading this book. At the very least, you know in your heart that you want more, even if you haven't quite figured out how to pull it off.

But maybe a better question would be: why bother?

In a world as busy as ours, filled with endless to-do lists and never enough time to-do them, why on earth would we take the time and energy to light a candle and just sit there or walk outside simply to look at the stars?

I thought you'd never ask.

Why It's Worth the Effort

There are plenty of reasons, but here are the ones I consider to be the most important.

Recharging the Battery

As I said before, all the running around we do takes a toll on us—body, mind, and spirit. Obviously, there are things we can do to support our bodies (eat well, exercise, get enough sleep), but let's face it, most of us don't do nearly as well with this group of things as we'd like to, no matter how good our intentions. (If you're guilty of this, raise your hand. *the author raises her hand*) Our minds usually have plenty to occupy them, but very little of that is quiet or joyful or refreshing. One way to keep going is to make sure that spirit gets some time and attention. It's like filling a psychic gas tank to help power the rest of your life.

Connecting with Nature

One of the problems of our modern world is that most of us are pretty far removed from "real" life. Unless you live in the country, you can go a long time without being someplace where you are truly surrounded by green, growing things. Light pollution blocks out the stars, and hardly anyone grows their own food anymore. Ancient Pagans developed their religions to help them understand and deal with the natural world, which had so much influence on their existence. In some ways, we modern Witches are the opposite: we developed our religions to help us get back in touch with a natural world that has become increasingly distant. On some level, most of us yearn to make that connection. Taking time for spirit can help us to do that.

Respect for the Gods

Nobody likes to be ignored. It isn't good manners to only connect with the gods when you want something or when things are going wrong. Just like your relationships with people, the better the relationship you build with the gods, the more likely they are to pay attention to you when you *do* need to call on them for help.

You Deserve It

This might be the most important reason of them all. Most of us spend the majority of our time and energy doing things for others—at work and at home, we are often trying to fulfill obligations, keep up with responsibilities, and make others happy. It is **REALLY IMPORTANT** to set aside a few moments here and there for yourself.

For one thing, we all need that to stay sane (or, in my case, kinda-sorta sane). For another, I think it is vital to send ourselves the message that we are worth taking time for. Nurturing spirit nurtures the essential you, and that, in turn, allows you to nurture others. If you only do things for others and never for yourself, sooner or later you are going to end up resenting them, and that's not good for anyone. So repeat after me: I *am worth taking time to nurture. I will make time for spirit.*

Five-Minute Rituals

"But I don't have time!" I hear you cry. Not to worry; all you need is five minutes. I've come up with a series of mini rituals that you literally can do in five minutes or less. So put down the cell phone, walk away from the Internet, and give yourself five minutes to do one or more of these every day (if you can manage it) or as often as possible (if you can't). Remember that the key to making these mini rituals work is the same as for any ritual: focus on what you are trying to achieve, then direct all your energy into the task. You can do that for five minutes; I know you can!

You can start with the quick rituals I talked about in chapter 2 or use the others listed here:

Greet the Day

Stand in front of a window and look out on the new day. Notice the weather and thank it for whatever it brings (even if it is something you don't like). Try to find something beautiful or positive to look at, even if it is just the light or a bird. Thank the gods for the new day. Open your heart to the possibilities it holds. Send out love into the world in general (it can use all it can get) and to those who are special to you. Don't forget to send some love to yourself, too. Put your hands over your heart and feel blessed.

Shower Away the Negative

We all have "stuff" we carry around that we don't want; some of it is ours, some of it we pick up from those around us (especially if you are someone who is particularly sensitive, which many Pagans are), not to mention illness and pain, depression, discouragement, and lots of negativity from both our own heads and the world around us. A quick ritual to rid ourselves of some of that crap is simply to stand under a running shower and visualize all that nasty stuff being washed away by the water and running down the drain. You might want to "see" the water drops surrounded by a glowing white or yellow light, then visualize yourself at the end of the shower clean and glowing inside and out. If you want to, you can say something like "stress and pain go down the drain; leave me feeling good again" or "I wash away negativity, opening myself up to light and love and all things good and beneficial."

Quick Protection Work

Whether you are walking into an unpleasant work environment or happen to get stuck sitting next to someone creepy on the bus, there are always times when you wish you'd had time to do a serious protection ritual or had remembered to redo that charm you stuck in your pocket. Here is a fast and easy ritual you can use in most situations at a moment's notice. Close your eyes briefly (if you're driving or in a meeting or something, do the best you can with your eyes open) and visualize yourself surrounded by a glowing white light. Inside the bubble of light, feel the love and protection of the Goddess (and/or God). On the outside, visualize a mirror facing outward, reflecting back whatever negativity is coming in your direction. Try not to send that energy back with resentment or fear; the more love and empathy you can put into this, the better it works.

Handy "Welcome Home" Cleansing

An easy way to keep from bringing all the nasty stuff from the outside world into your home is to put a bowl of water somewhere near your front door. Whenever you come back home, take a moment to stop and rinse your hands in the water. (You might want to keep a towel nearby, but you can also just dip your fingertips if there isn't room for one.) Visualize anything unpleasant being drained off into the water. You'll need to change the water periodically, as it will get darker over time.

Steam Things Up

Here's a really fast way to bless your home and affirm your faith. Every time you take a shower, draw a pentacle (or the symbol of your choice) in the steam on the window or mirror. Visualize the symbol glowing for a moment, marking your space as magickal. Once the steam is gone, no one will know it is there but you.

Embrace Yourself

We often feel alone and vulnerable, and some people don't have nearly enough love in their lives. But the Goddess/God loves us all. If you need a hug, give yourself one, and feel yourself embraced by the love of the gods as you do so.

Touch Nature

It doesn't matter if you literally hug a tree or walk out into the rain or stop to smell a flower. Take five minutes to really pay attention to nature. If you don't have anything natural around you, simply eat an apple. Just do it slowly and mindfully, being aware of the scent, the feel of the juices in your mouth, the texture of the tough skin and the crisp insides. In your mind's eye, see the tree the apple came from, the blossom it began as, the rain that nurtured it, and the soil that helped it grow until it was ripe so that you could eat it. Feel that part of you that is now being nurtured by that natural energy of the apple.

Bless and Consecrate

You can bless and consecrate anything: magickal tools, kitchen implements, your garden, your car, your cat (if you can get said cat to sit still enough—good luck with that). I like to bless and consecrate the magickal necklaces I make, any new tools (especially candles), and anything else that gets used in any way in my magickal life. All you need are items that represent the elements of earth, air, water, and fire, and maybe something to represent God/dess. For earth I usually use salt, but you can also use a crystal or even some dirt. For air I usually use the smoke from a sage smudge stick, but a feather also works well, or incense. Water...well, that's pretty self-explanatory. And for fire I like to use a lit candle, although the smudge stick or incense can always do double duty.

Just assemble the four items you are going to use, and maybe another candle or a statue for God/dess (I have a small kit I keep together so all I have to do is grab it and be ready in a second), and the item you want to bless and consecrate. Sprinkle the item with salt (or wave the crystal over it), saying, "I bless and consecrate you with the power of earth," and repeat with the other three elements. If you are using something to represent the Goddess and/or God, say:

> I ask God/dess to bless this _____ so that I might use it for magickal
> and positive work. So mote it be.

And there you go!

Say Thank You

It doesn't matter what for. Take five minutes out of your busy day to send gratitude out into the universe. Thank the gods for the good stuff. If you can, thank them for the bad stuff, too (which usually teaches us something, even if it isn't fun to go through). Just be grateful for five minutes a day. It will open up your heart in amazing ways.

Look Up

At some time before you go to bed, look out at the sky. Go outside and look up if you can. If you can't, look out a window. The stars and moon are up there, even if you live in a place where they are hard to see. Feel how big the universe is and remember that you are made of the same things that stars are made of. Say goodnight to the moon. If you want, send out a little prayer.

Daily Divination

Lots of people read their horoscope every morning, but for many of us, that is the only bit of "checking in" we do. After all, few people have the time or inclination to do a full tarot spread with their morning coffee. And mostly, we don't need that much detailed information. Luckily, there are lots of fast and easy ways to get a quick hint at what your day holds or what you need to know to make the most of it.

Years ago, when I was practicing with my first coven, the high priestess had us do an interesting experiment. Every day for a month, we pulled one rune stone at the beginning of the day. We wrote down the stone and any flashes of intuition we got when we looked at it, then checked in at the end of the day to see if there was, in fact, any relationship between the two. Not surprisingly, there often was.

This also turned out to be a great way of learning the runes themselves. I started out having to look up the meanings of each rune in a book (my favorite is Lisa Peschel's A *Practical Guide to the Runes*—it's old, but it is easy to use and understand), but by the end of the month, I was much more familiar with them. If you're interested in becoming better acquainted with the stones or any other form of divination, try doing something like this. It's a fun and practical way to learn. Either pull one out of a bag, if that's what you store them in, or place them in a small bowl and just close your eyes and grab one.

If rune stones aren't your thing, you can do this with tarot cards instead. If you're not used to using the cards, I suggest starting with something basic like the classic Rider-Waite Tarot. That's the one I started with lo these many years ago, and I have been reading professionally for ages with this one pack. It's a bit battered by now, but it works so well for me that I'm rarely tempted to switch to something else, despite the bevy of beautiful decks out there. However, there are lots of variations on the tarot card deck, and you can pick whichever one seems to speak to you most loudly.

As with the rune stones, you can start your day by shuffling the deck and picking out a card at random. Sometimes one will even jump out of the deck for you. You can either ask a question (What does my day hold? What do I need to know today?) or just see what comes up. If you are dealing with something tricky, you can ask a specific question, like "Should I go out on a date with that hunky guy at the office?"

There are plenty of alternatives for those who don't have or like either rune stones or tarot cards. I have a number of interesting decks that I use for inspiration, answers, or just as a way to get in touch with spirit quickly and easily.

One of my favorites, which I've used numerous times in ritual with my group Blue Moon Circle, is the *Goddess Inspiration Oracle* by Kris Waldherr. She's well known for her beautiful goddess-themed artwork, and this deck is filled with amazing images, as well as lovely descriptions of the eighty goddesses featured on the cards—yet another way to learn while being inspired and guided.

Another one I like is *The Gifts of the Goddess: 36 Affirmation Cards* by Amy Zerner and Monte Farber.

My current favorite was a Yule gift from my friend Rebecca Elson. She gets to preview lots of great decks for her blog The Magical Buffet, and she knew I'd love this one when she saw it. *The Conscious Spirit Oracle Deck* by Kim Dreyer has lovely pictures and inspiring affirmations. I've taken to pulling one each morning, standing at my altar, and reading it out loud. Then I try to carry its message through the rest of my day. For instance, this morning's card was number 18: Air Elemental, with the affirmation "I embrace the element of air and am open to all knowledge and wisdom."

Isn't that a great way to start out the day? (Also, I have to do research today, so it makes a certain amount of sense.)

You can also use one of the simplest forms of divination there is: a pendulum. I have a nice one with an amethyst crystal dangling off the bottom, but it is easy to make a homemade pendulum, too. All you need is a chain or strong thread and something to hang off of it that will be reasonably lightweight and well balanced. Pendulums are relatively limited—they work best with yes or no questions—but they do work. To use one, first you need to find out which way it swings for yes and which way for no (some go left to right, others circle around clockwise or counterclockwise). To do this, ask a yes or no question you know the answer to, like "Is my name Deborah?" and see how the pendulum moves. Hold the string or chain loosely between a couple of fingers and allow the pendant at the bottom to hang freely. Then ask your questions.

The simplest way to use any of these options is to choose one—runes or tarot or some other form of tapping into your intuition—and simply pull one stone or card each morning. Take a minute to focus on it, and you're done.

If you want to take it a step further, you can keep a couple of different options out where you can access them easily and pull from whichever one calls to you the most that day, or do runes one month and tarot cards another.

To go a little deeper—and I highly recommend trying this sometime, at least for a month—write down your stone or card and any thoughts or feelings you have about it, and keep track of them in a small notebook or in your Book of Shadows, if you have one. (If you already journal, you can add this to your daily jottings.) At the end of a day, a week, or a month, take a look back and see if you can make out any patterns that could be helpful.

You can also keep a dream journal. Sometimes hints for the future come to us in our dreams, especially if we put a dream sachet under the pillow and go to bed with the intention of dreaming in a deep and meaningful way.

Asking for guidance and/or inspiration doesn't have to be complicated or take a lot of time. You certainly don't have to be an expert card reader to do it. (In fact, many folks like me who read professionally can't read for themselves at all. Ironic, isn't it?) You just have to take the same amount of time and effort you would put into reading your daily horoscope. And honestly, this is likely to be a lot more helpful!

The Hibernation Vacation

I haven't taken a real vacation in years. I've gone to a fair amount of conventions and conferences, including Pantheacon (a big Pagan convention in San Jose), the Romance Writers of America national conference in New York City and Washington DC, and a few smaller writing conferences. These trips are definitely fun and a great change of pace from my regular life, but make no mistake: they're work, not vacation.

The closest thing to a vacation I've had was probably four or five years ago, the last time the Blue Moon Circle gang (and families) took a three-day weekend and went to the Sterling Renaissance Faire. We used to do that almost every year, dressing up and going to the Faire by day and sitting by the fire drinking wine and laughing by night. It was simple, fun, and relaxing. But people's schedules have gotten tighter and, of course, there's that whole money thing.

The truth is, it can be hard to find the time and money to take a real vacation, as much as we might all want to go sit on the beach with a good book, a fruity drink with an umbrella in it, and a cute cabana boy. (Wait, maybe that's just me.) But it doesn't mean that our bodies and spirits don't need a break from the stresses and strains of everyday life. So this year, I'm planning to take a hibernation vacation.

And yes, I just made that up. But feel free to borrow the idea and use it yourself in whichever way works best for you.

Here's how I envision the hibernation vacation:

For one thing, I'll be doing it at home—way cheaper that way and, in some ways, more relaxing. No packing, no traveling, and no worries about forgetting something important…

For another, the plan is to do less instead of more. Most vacations involve running around like crazy, trying to cram as much as possible into the time you have. The hibernation vacation is all about UN-cramming your life.

The general idea is to remove as much of the daily pressure of life as possible. For instance, I normally write every day, for at least a few hours in the evening. For the duration of my hibernation vacation, I'm going to give myself permission not to do that. If I get an idea, I can jot it down; I can play with plans for future work. But no doing the work itself until later.

I will still have to go into work (although if you can actually manage to do this on a weekend or take a couple days off, even better), but I'm not going to worry too much about running a million errands on the way home. And I'll be saying no to all social activities and requests from others.

When I am home, I am going to focus on reconnecting with my spiritual practice and my physical well-being. I will eat better, exercise more, and meditate. I also want to focus more energy on my magickal practice instead of just writing about it. (Yes, I see the irony there.)

There are also things I've been saying I was going to do—such as re-learning to play guitar and crochet—which never seem to make it to the top of the to-do list. The hibernation vacation is the perfect space in time to allow myself to recharge my creative batteries by doing things that aren't "work" creativity (like writing or jewelry making) but things I do just for me, just for fun.

A shocking idea, isn't it!

These days, we all tend to be focused on what has to be done for others or what we need to do to ensure our everyday survival and pay the bills. It is too easy to forget to fill the well we draw from every day—and then, when we hit a point where the well is empty, we can't figure out why.

A hibernation vacation is a way to give yourself the gift of time: recharge your internal battery and hit the reboot button on some of your daily patterns that could use shaking up. It doesn't have to be a whole week. Take a weekend, if that's all you can spare, or even just a day. My friend Robin, who is married with kids and runs a daycare, lives for the rare times when her hubby takes the kids out for the whole day and she gets to be all by herself and *not cleaning anything*. She takes a long bath, reads a book, and actually sits down—a mini hibernation vacation that gives her a break from the constant need to always be there for someone else.

Turn off your phone, stay off the Internet, only watch fun things on the TV (no news, for Goddess's sake!). Read a book. Make a list of the things you want to do for yourself that you never have time for, and then do them. And don't forget to focus on your spiritual practice, whatever that might be. Go out at night and look at the stars. Listen to the rain or the sound of the waves. Or turn everything off and listen to the silence.

Then you can listen to yourself, and that's what a hibernation vacation is all about.

Making Time for Spirit
MICKIE MUELLER

I've been a pretty busy Witch since I began on this magical path. I've gone from being a working mom with two jobs while dreaming of a budding art career to being a full-time executive Witch, artist, writer, head cook, and groundskeeper of several acres. How on earth have I managed to fit spiritual practice into all of that? I do it with planning, thinking ahead, and making every task a magical one.

I've found that when I add magic into my everyday activities, I have Spirit in every part of my day. Cleaning, cooking, and even when I'm writing and illustrating, I've found ways to add magic to everything I do. After all, being a Witch isn't just something we do; it's who we are. I add herbal infusions and a few drops of oils to my body wash, shampoo, and conditioner, and then I work a spell to activate them for cleansing away negativity and boosting my energy field. One spell lasts through every shower!

I enchant my cup of coffee or tea, making it a small ritual depending on what I need that day. It might be extra energy, centering myself, or embracing the spirit of love. I choose a cup that represents my spiritual goal, and then I quickly trace magical symbols above the cup of my brew, whispering my needs into the cup. It's powerful magic because it activates the herbs becoming part of every cell in my body, but it only takes a few minutes. Some varieties of tea I use for specific goals. For instance, chamomile lavender is usually my go-to tea when I need to relax or calm jangled nerves. For specific teas, I enchant the entire box—then the magic is already done and infuses with the hot water as the tea brews.

I've charmed my everyday cleaning broom to sweep away negativity along with dust and dirt. I started using one of those mops with the container of cleaning fluid right on it, and I make my own fluid. I fill it with an enchanted herbal infusion with vinegar and water, a magical floor wash to banish negativity and bring love, prosperity, and protection into my home. I make the wash once, do the spell, and it lasts until the next refill. The idea here is to work smarter, not harder; I'm always coming up with ways to plan ahead and get the most out of my magic.

I have several permanent altars that I use on a regular basis. They keep the energy flowing, and everything I need is right there. I have a creativity altar on my art table. The healing altar in my home is a sacred space I use for the quick and easy answering of healing requests. I try to honor the God and Goddess in every corner of my home; in this way, Spirit radiates out and I keep my magic and my connection to Spirit active all the time.

Walking Your Talk
in Everyday Life

Following our spiritual beliefs is part of living a life that makes us feel satisfied and fulfilled. While these beliefs are different for everyone, what we all share is the need to find ways to integrate our spiritual beliefs as Wiccans, Witches, and Pagans into our everyday lives as busy human beings. Sometimes we fall short; that's the human bit. But it can be easier than you think to walk your talk every day.

Awareness, Appreciation, and Attitude

Part of being a Witch or a Pagan means that we look at the world slightly differently than most folks. To me, this comes down to three basic things: awareness, appreciation, and attitude. Because we follow a nature-based religion, we tend to have a greater awareness and appreciation of the natural world around us, and our attitude toward it is one of gratitude and nurturing as opposed to merely taking it for granted or even believing that it exists simply for our use, regardless of the consequences. (I'm not saying that this approach is limited to Pagans, by the way. More and more people are starting to develop a greater awareness of the fragility and value of the planet.)

But, as with everything else, these three things sometimes get lost in the shuffle, and it often takes a metaphorical smack upside the head to remind us of their importance.

Let use consider, for instance, the price of water.

What is the price of water? At my house recently, it was $2,400—a rather large sum of money to deal with a rather small problem (tiny iron bacteria in my 340-foot-deep well, which, while harmless to humans, make the water smell and taste bad and build up gunk inside pipes and appliances, all while staining everything they touch a charming reddish-brown). The money was to treat the water and then filter it.

It wasn't fun to hand over all that cash, but it got me thinking about the price of water. Most of us, me included, tend to think that water is free. After all, it can be found just lying around in lakes, streams, and oceans, and it falls from the sky as rain. If you turn on your faucet, water comes out. What could be easier?

True, if you own a house in a city or town, you will probably pay some kind of water tax—essentially paying the city to make sure that the water is clean and safe to drink, and doesn't have nasty little critters like iron bacteria in it. Folks like me who live in the country sometimes have to pay to have a well dug if there isn't one on the property or if the one you have runs dry.

But that's not the real cost of water. When I started really thinking about it, I realized that in our modern world, there are all sorts of hidden costs, many of which our ancestors never dealt with.

Not that water came without a price for them—on the contrary, they were well aware of how precious it was. If they wanted water to drink, they carried it by hand from wells or used pumps that required actual muscle. If the rains were scarce, they irrigated their fields by hand, dragging water from nearby sources if they had them. And there was no guarantee that there would be water for crops or even to drink. Little wonder that they prized water as one of the four great elements and prayed to gods who controlled the weather.

These days we don't have to work nearly as hard for our water, but that very fact has led us to disconnect ourselves from the price we pay to have our modern lifestyle. We have polluted many of our precious sources of water with factory runoff and chemical fertilizers (not just from huge factory farms, either, but also from smaller farms and regular folks who want perfect lawns).

And then there are the manufacturing plants. According to the World Wildlife Federation, "It can take more than 20,000 litres of water to produce 1kg of cotton; equivalent to a single T-shirt and pair of jeans" (see http://wwf.panda.org/about_our_earth/about_freshwater/freshwater_problems/thirsty_crops/cotton/). That's a pretty pricey outfit.

One of the hot-button topics these days, especially in upstate New York where I live, is fracking—hydraulic fracturing, which is a technique used to access natural gas in shale deposits under the surface of the land. Fracking uses many poisonous chemicals, and the natural gas itself can end up breaking through and contaminating the groundwater in a huge area surrounding the wells. Most people know that and either think it is plenty safe or very dangerous, depending on which side of the argument they come down on. But what you hardly hear anyone talk about is the fact that the process uses thousands of gallons of water—which is then too contaminated to be used again for drinking or crops.

Much of the United States is currently in the middle of an ongoing drought that shows no sign of ending anytime soon. Farmers and ranchers in the Midwest are at risk of losing everything, and the loss of corn crops and cattle have already driven up the cost of food. There's a price to that water as well. Droughts have decimated other countries too, especially those of developing countries. It is estimated that over a billion people across the world don't have access to clean, drinkable water.

Human beings have built huge cities on what was previously uninhabitable desert land. My parents and sister live in San Diego, a beautiful city where 50 percent of their water is brought in from the Colorado River, another 30 percent comes from the Bay-Delta in Northern California, and a mere 20 percent comes from local supplies. According to the San Diego

County Water Authority, "Local surface water runoff from rainfall is an important part of the San Diego region's water supply, but it hasn't provided enough water to meet all of the region's needs since 1947" (see http://www .sdcwa.org/san-diego-county-water-sources).

There are plenty of other examples for how human beings are using and abusing this precious natural resource, but I think you see my point. Water isn't really free after all. There is a price of water attached to every action we take and every decision we make in our day-to-day life.

The point of all this musing, brought on by my own unexpected confrontation with the hidden realities of dealing with water, was not to depress you. It's not a political statement of any kind or even an environmental rant. (Although believe me, I could give you one of those if you wanted it.)

It's nothing more than a gentle reminder that in our own way, we are as dependent on the precious element of water as our ancestors were. And although we may have easier access and the ability to move water to the places where we want it—some of the time, within serious limitations— this only increases our need to use it wisely.

We can all do this in little ways every day with very little sacrifice. Here are a few easy ways to cut your use of water, thereby walking your talk with a greater awareness:

- Buy your produce from organic farmers who don't use chemical fertilizers.

- Instead of getting new clothes each time you want a new outfit, pick up something gently used from a consignment store.

- Cut down on wasteful use of water: take shorter showers, fix any leaky faucets, don't let the water run constantly while washing dishes, replace old toilets with new low-flow models.

- Keep your own water sources as clean and protected as possible.

- Don't try to grow the perfect lawn, and focus on plants that grow naturally in your area, since they are usually designed to work in that particular ecosystem.

- If you garden, try collecting rainwater in a barrel to use for irrigation.

- Do a little research and become better educated about the price of water in the modern world.

- Join or contribute to organizations that clean and protect rivers, lakes, and oceans.

- Contribute to organizations that help people in developing countries have access to clean, drinkable water. (In many of the poorer parts of the world, there is no clean water—everything is contaminated with parasites, sewage, or something else that can cause serious illness or even death. Since it is all they have, these folks have no choice but to drink the water and use it on their crops.)

As Pagans, I believe we have a responsibility to be mindful of the planet we live on and of how we treat its gifts—earth, air, fire, and water among them. We can't always change the big-picture issues (although we can certainly try), but we can be more conscious about our own patterns and choices.

Yes, there are many ways in which water is free and readily accessible, and that is a wonderful thing. But in some ways it also comes with a cost, and not just if you happen to have iron-eating parasites in your well.

This is true of many of the other modern conveniences we take for granted. Being mindful of that fact doesn't mean that we can't enjoy the good things life has to offer or that we need to feel guilty whenever we turn on the faucet or an electric light. However, it can easily become part of your daily Witchcraft practice to be more aware and more appreciative, and to balance your own needs and wants against what is good for the planet.

Here are a few simple steps you can take if you want to walk your talk as a nature worshiper just a little bit more.

Change the Way You Eat

There are a couple of easy ways to reduce your negative impact on the environment by making simple changes in how you eat. For instance, buy locally grown foods when you can. Not only will you be supporting local farmers, but food grown locally doesn't have to be shipped across the country (or, often, from completely different countries); this applies to eating food that is in season in your area as well. For instance, I love asparagus, but I usually only eat it during the few months a year that it is in season in my region. (Bonus: eating food in season is usually also cheaper.) I'm not suggesting that you only eat foods grown near where you live—in that case, I would never be able to have a citrus fruit or an avocado—but try making the switch with some of the foods you eat.

Additionally, if you are not already a vegetarian, you may want to consider eating less meat. Everyone has to make his or her own decision about whether or not to eat meat at all, but there are lots of good reasons to do so in moderation. Raising meat is tough on the environment; it takes a lot of water and grain to produce one pound of beef, and the animals themselves give off a sizable amount of the greenhouse gasses that contribute to global warming (see http://michaelbluejay.com/veg/environment.html). I eat meat, but usually only a few times a month, and I try to buy organic, free range, and/or local meat that I know has been raised humanely. I am also mindful of the sacrifice of the animal and try to eat with appreciation and gratitude for that sacrifice.

Use Less Energy

Everyone knows the basics of using less energy: turn off lights in unoccupied rooms, don't leave the TV on for hours with no one watching, unplug small appliances that continually suck energy while they aren't in use, carpool or walk or bike to work, and all the rest. Hopefully you're already doing some of those things. (For a good resource for more suggestions, go to 101 Ways to Save Energy at Powerhouse TV.com, http://www .powerhousetv.com/Energy-EfficientLiving/Energy-savingsTips/027471.)

But just because we know how to do it doesn't mean we always follow through. As a part of your spiritual practice, why not have a goal of adding one energy-saving habit every month?

Raise Your Children to Be Aware and Appreciative

Children learn from the adults around them. I am constantly impressed by my friends who are raising their children as Pagans by walking their talk every day and providing good examples of how to be mindful and connect with the earth. If we want the next generation to treat the earth well, it has to start with us and then get passed on to the next generation.

Become Active in Environmental Causes

There are a number of Pagans who are especially known for their involvement with environmental causes. Starhawk (author of *The Spiral Dance*) is probably the most famous. On her activism website, she says, "Because I believe the earth is a living being, because we are all part of that life, because every human being embodies the Goddess, because I have a fierce, passionate love for redwoods and ravens, because clear running water is sacred, I'm an activist." She also lists a number of environmental causes that she and other Pagans are currently involved in (see http://www .starhawk.org/activism/activism.html). Some are gathering together (both in the United States and the United Kingdom) to fight fracking. Others protest clear-cutting the forests or hunting animals like wolves that are in danger of extinction and whose deaths throw the natural world out of balance. Pick a cause you believe in and become involved on whatever level you can manage. Not everyone is going to join a march or chain themselves to a tree, but everyone can sign petitions, write a letter to their congressperson, or send five dollars to an organization that does work to support the environment.

Be aware of what is going on in the world around you, be appreciative of the gifts we have been given, and maintain an attitude of gratitude as part of your ongoing spiritual practice. Witchcraft means looking both within and without.

CHAPTER 4

Service as Sacred Work

I have to confess that I have always admired priests and monks and nuns. Whether they're Catholic, Buddhist, or any other faith, I truly respect people who live lives that are dedicated to prayer and service. Some of these folks go places that no one else wants to go and do jobs that no one else is willing to, from tending to lepers to feeding the homeless in frightening neighborhoods. For most, service to others is considered to be a part of their religious practice—"doing the work of god."

I'm not about to don a habit (although I do look good in black), but I have always believed that doing things for others is an important part of creating a life with value and meaning. And I like to think that, at least in this area, I do pretty well at walking my talk.

Take my day job, for instance. I run a not-for-profit artists' cooperative shop that a friend and I started back in 1999. We saw a need in our town for a place for local artisans to sell their work and for people to be able to shop for beautiful handcrafted items they could actually afford. We purposely found a place on the main street for the store because, like so many other small towns, our downtown was suffering.

We created this place to serve the artists, the community, and the town (and, to some extent, ourselves, since I make jewelry and my friend makes pottery). And since the store opened, a number of other small towns in the region have followed in our footsteps and started similar endeavors. Since we're still around, I'd say we're a success.

I love my job. It has its good sides (fifty artists and a flexible schedule) and its bad sides (fifty artists and a lot of paperwork). It doesn't pay particularly well, but it does satisfy my need to be doing something that is of service to others. My college degrees were in psychology and, later, secondary English education, so you can see that was always an important part of my motivation. Maybe I was a monk in another life.

Not everyone is going to have a career that involves service to others, although plenty do (nurses and teachers, for instance). But there are plenty of ways to perform acts of service in your daily life, doing the work of Goddess with every small deed that helps another.

Friends and Family

You may have heard the expression "charity begins at home." What this means, basically, is that before you worry about giving to the world outside, first look around you to see if there is anyone close to you who needs help. My first priority is always my friends and family; even if I am facing a writing deadline, I try to make sure I have time to listen if a friend is in crisis. If you are thinking about being of service, look first at those who are closest to you. Does a family member need something you can give? Is there an elderly neighbor who could use a hand? If you think you don't have any extra time or energy for volunteer work, try looking closer to home to see what you can do for others.

Coming to the Aid of Children

Children are essentially helpless—there is little they can do for themselves if they are in distress—and yet the rewards for helping them are limitless. You can come to the aid of children in large ways (adopting or fostering a child, for instance), but there are also smaller things that most of us can do: become a Big Brother or Big Sister, mentor a child you know, or volunteer at a local school, library, or hospital (some hospitals need people simply to cuddle babies with AIDS, Fetal Alcohol Syndrome, or other issues). Work with the Girl Scouts, Boy Scouts, or some local organization. Investing in a child's well-being is like investing in the future.

Helping the Less Fortunate

Most of us aren't wealthy, but at least we have a roof over our heads and food on the table. Not everyone is so lucky. There always have been people in our society who have fallen through the cracks; since the economy started its downward slide, there are more than ever. Some of these folks have drug, alcohol, or mental illness issues. Some of them are veterans who had a hard time making the transition back to civilian life. Others are just regular people who lost their jobs and haven't been able to find new ones. No matter how rough we might have it, there is always somebody else who is worse off. One way to show the gods your appreciation for what you have is to help those who haven't been as fortunate. Volunteer at a soup kitchen. If you have a garden that produces more than you can eat, many local soup kitchens and pantries will happily accept your extra fruits and vegetables. Instead of throwing out clothes or items you no longer use, donate them to the Salvation Army or a local organization that helps the community. If you want to teach your children an appreciation for what they have, you may be able to find a place where you can volunteer as a family.

Assisting the Old and Sick

It is tough to be old in our society. Pagans tend to have a respect for the "crone" and the elders that isn't always shared by the general population. What better way to show this than to work with the elderly? If you can spare a couple of hours every month, read to someone who can no longer read for himself. What about going to the hospital or a nursing home and spending a little time with someone whose family lives too far away to visit or who has no family at all? Some nursing homes will allow pet visits, which can really cheer up the residents, so if you have an animal that does well around fragile people, you might want to look into that.

Turning Crafts into Gifts

Maybe you don't have time (or the inclination) to do volunteer work; not everyone does. Do you do a craft that can be turned into a useful gift for someone else? One of the women in Blue Moon Circle is an avid knitter. She has made special caps to go inside soldier's helmets, and blankets that are used to wrap babies that tragically don't get to go home from the hospital. I've even seen people online talking about knitting sweaters for penguins whose feathers have been damaged by oil spills. Every year, some of the banks and churches here have "mitten trees," where people can donate mittens they've made for people who need them. Don't knit? Maybe there is some other way the craft you do for fun can benefit others. I often donate my handcrafted jewelry when organizations are having auctions to raise money for good causes, for instance.

Nurturing Nature

And let's not forget about Mother Nature. As Witches and Pagans, it makes sense that some of our acts of service be directed at helping the planet. If you belong to a coven, maybe you would like to band together and adopt a stretch of highway to clean. Or you can just do what my friend Ellen and I do: when we take her dogs for a walk down the country road I live on, we bring a bag to put empty bottles and other garbage in, cleaning as we go. If you have a yard, you can plant trees and shrubs that produce berries that feed the birds and other critters, or put out birdseed (especially in the winter, when food is scarce). Other things you can do if you have a home in the country or in the suburbs is to put up bat houses, birdhouses, or bee shelters.

Can't plant anything where you live? Donate a few dollars to the Arbor Day Foundation and have them plant trees for you. If you live in the city, there is something called "guerrilla gardening." This is where you plant seeds in abandoned, derelict, or otherwise unattractive places, sometimes using seed bombs created from soil and seeds wetted just enough to hold them together into a ball. I'm not advocating doing anything illegal (I'd hate to be responsible for one of my readers ending up in jail), but there are plenty of places where you can beautify the neighborhood in the name of Gaia without getting into trouble.

Aiding Animals

Like children, animals are essentially powerless in our society. Pagans and Witches often feel a special bond with animals, so maybe this is an area where we might take that bond and turn it to service. If you are looking for a new pet, consider adopting one from a shelter instead of buying a purebred. If there is a particular breed you have your heart set on, check to see if there is a rescue organization for that breed (these organizations place abandoned or misused pets). Can't have a pet on a permanent basis but still want to help? Some shelters look for people to foster kittens and their mothers until they are old enough to go to forever homes. You can train service dogs or volunteer at a local shelter.

No time? How about donating old blankets and towels to shelters or the vet, or chipping in a few dollars to support efforts to spay and neuter feral cats?

And Everything Else

If none of these ideas appeal to you, there is always *something* you can do as an act of service. Donate blood, do literacy training, sign petitions—whatever works for your schedule, suits your lifestyle, and fills your heart with joy. It is my sincere belief that the gods put us here on earth to help and comfort each other, and that when we do so, we get back much more than we gave out. So consider what you can do to be of service, as an "act of Goddess," and then go out and do it. Your Mother would be proud.

Walking Your Talk Every Day

It doesn't really matter what you do or how you do it. We each have different styles and approaches to our practice of the Craft. Some people will be more adventurous and some, quite tame. Some can practice out in the open and others have to find ways to disguise their magickal doings. Whether you practice alone or with a coven or with your entire immediate family, what is truly important is that you practice.

Walking your talk every day doesn't have to mean doing formal ritual or dedicating a special room in your house to magickal work or wearing the world's largest pentacle. It merely entails finding ways to integrate your beliefs as a Witch and a Pagan into your life in meaningful and heartfelt ways. If you see recycling and composting as a gift to the Goddess, then even taking out the garbage can be a spiritual endeavor.

Being an everyday Witch is more about attitude and heart than anything else. How you go about it is completely up to you.

Sharing My Witchy Life
ASHLEEN O'GAEA

I've been sharing my witchy life since 1987, and I'm still at it. Over the years I've written articles, essays, chapters, forwards, stories, and books. Most of my readers have been Pagan or already interested in Paganism.

I helped found the Tucson Area Wiccan-Pagan Network in the late 1980s, and as a TAWN representative I have made a number of radio, television, and other public appearances. After twenty-five years of intense involvement I retired, though I'm still a member and still subscribe and contribute to TAWN's newsletter, *Tapestry*.

For the last thirteen years (so far), I've been the senior writing priestess for Mother Earth Ministries-ATC, a Neopagan prison ministry based in Tucson. With our founder Carol Garr, I co-authored *Enchantment Encumbered: The Study and Practice of Wicca in Restricted Environments*, written especially for incarcerated Wiccans. I write virtually all of MEM's brochures and flyers, and answer between one and two hundred letters a month from inmates all over the country.

I'm retired from the nine-to-five, don't ride the city bus anymore, and am finding ways to spend less than five days a week writing for MEM so that I have time for more of a personal life. Mind you, I'm still living the witchy life: I'm an ordained priestess; my husband-priest and I still do handfastings (most of them legal weddings) and other rites of passage. We belong to a coven in the tradition we founded. We host sabbat celebrations, some of which are at various campsites around southeastern Arizona, and we teach Adventure Wicca 101 classes once a year and help the coven's priestess train dedicants. Still, it's nice to have time for other things, including exploring our Scottish ancestry. We've started going to Celtic festivals and Highland Games, and in 2013, for the first time, we represented our Scottish clan with a booth at the Tucson Games. Earlier that year we went to an out-of-state festival, and that's where the gods showed us our next venue.

We're a small clan, so even though our booths get quite a few visitors, not many of them are kin. When a tall, elegant, well-spoken Southern woman introduced herself as a kinswoman, I naturally handed her a business card. Now we have cards that picture us in tartan, with our contact info on one side and clan info on the other.

Then what I had was a card for my consulting business, and it had a pentagram on it. The lady took it, and the pentagram held her gaze. She began to tremble, and then, in a strangled sort of church-lady voice, she thrust the card back at me. "I don't need this card," she said.

Bless me, it took a second to figure out what the problem was. "Oh, I'm not pitching my business," I said. "It's just what I have with my contact info."

"No, I don't want this card," she insisted.

Ahhh. The pentagram.

I don't remember exactly what the next few lines of conversation were. I was befuddled. I was in priestess mode because I wanted to comfort this woman, obviously terrified by the "devil-star," and, honestly, I wanted to defend myself. I explained to her that I wasn't giving her the card to convert her and that we don't do that. "It's just because we're kinswomen," I emphasized, "and we're a small clan, so we should keep in touch."

She kept the card.

It seems to me that the way I need to share my witchy life with non-Pagans now is to work on introducing Wicca to the Celtic Festival–Highland Games crowd. They're already pretty comfortable with Druidry, that being Irish; at the Tucson Games, the local Druids always have a booth. My husband and I bought a new festival tent because we want to hold clan booths at all four Arizona Games as the rest of our schedule allows. We can't make it all about the Paganism because, open-minded as they are, most of my clan are Christian. But I have an idea for a brochure, which might turn into a book…

Sharing one's witchy life with non-Pagans is always a challenge—sometimes a delicate one. We're on the threshold now of taking that sharing to another level, and we're already sure it's going to be both interesting—verrrrry interesting—and very worthwhile.

A Simple Pagan Practice

Bringing Nature into Your Life

There are many things that set a modern Pagan practice aside from most other religious paths. For one thing, most Witches worship a god and a goddess instead of only a patriarchal male god. For another, we believe that magick is real—a force in the universe that we can tap into and use for positive change. But although these things are certainly important aspects of being a Witch, there is one core tenet that we sometimes lose track of, despite the fact that it is often one of the things that drew us to Witchcraft in the first place.

Witchcraft is a nature-based religion. We follow the Wheel of the Year in its perpetual cycle of birth, growth, death, and rebirth, just as the natural world around us does. The waxing and waning of the moon is our guide for many of our endeavors. The four elements of earth, air, fire, and water play a pivotal role in many of our rituals.

And yet, many of us aren't nearly as in tune with nature as we'd like to be. This chapter is full of suggestions for how to change that.

....

Going with the Flow: Changing with Grace

I have lived in upstate New York my entire life. For the most part, I love it here. I love the changing seasons and the beauty of the rolling hills. What I don't love so much is winter, which is not a good thing in an area where the first snow often falls at Halloween and it isn't unheard of for it to snow in the middle of April. Essentially, of the twelve months in a year, five of them are winter. That's a long freaking time if you don't like that particular season.

For much of my life, I used to get seriously depressed during the winter. Some of this can be blamed on the lack of light or on not being able to spend much time outside in the fresh air. (I'm not a winter sports person… any activity that involves purposely subjecting oneself to freezing cold and snow is not my cup of hot chocolate.) But mostly I just didn't like winter. Cold, snow, sleet, ice, cold…bah.

These days, things are different. While I still count the days until spring, I rarely get the winter blues, and I find that there are some things about it I positively look forward to. What caused the change? I became a Pagan.

You are probably wondering why on earth that would make any difference—and if you live in a chilly part of the country, you may also be wondering if it could help your own winter blues, if you get them. It's pretty simple, really, and the reason I'm sharing this here is because I am hoping that, yes, it will help a few other folks turn things around.

One of the major changes that happened when I started a regular Witchcraft practice was that I learned to go with the flow of the seasons, living my life in tune with the ever-shifting Wheel of the Year. As I internalized this connection even more, I realized that a big part of my winter depression came from the fact that I was *fighting* the flow of the season instead of moving *with it*. It took a *lot* of energy to push while the earth was pulling, and it was a huge waste of psychic energy to be constantly wishing for the season to be something it wasn't.

Once I accepted winter for the natural part of the cycle it is, I was able to start appreciating some of its positive sides, which I hadn't recognized before becoming a Pagan and changing my view of the world.

Winter is a time of quiet—of turning inward and hibernating and being less outwardly focused and more inwardly focused. Once I realized this, I started to use that quiet internal time instead of fighting it. (In my case, because I run an artists' cooperative shop, my slow time doesn't really start until January...but that still gave me January, February, and March.) I gave myself permission to slow down instead of trying to force myself to have summer energy in the middle of winter. I focused on the quietly creative forces—usually writing a book during that three months' time, when it might have taken me four to six months during a busier, less quiet time of the year. I didn't socialize as much; I napped more and dreamed and planned for the more active seasons to come.

And gradually, I realized that I wasn't getting depressed anymore. I still don't exactly love winter. But I can look out the window and appreciate the beauty of the pristine white snow glistening on the trees and the bright red flash of a cardinal coming in to feast at the bird feeder outside my window. I know that eventually the Wheel will turn, bringing with it spring and warmth. And until then, I sink into the silence and slower pace of winter, and try to move with the flow instead of against it.

This story is just one example of how we can use the rhythms of nature to improve our own lives. The moral here is that it takes a lot less energy—and is usually much healthier—if we can go with the flow. Sometimes, as with me, this means you have to take a good look at your own patterns and attitudes, and figure out what's working and what's not. This can be difficult; it takes some tough self-love and the willingness to really be honest with yourself. But isn't it worth some work to feel better and live a happier, healthier life?

Many eons ago (in the mid to late eighties, long before I found my way to a Pagan path), I went out for a number of years with a very smart, very capable guy. We'll call him Bubba. Bubba had a lot going for him, but he was a really unhappy man. After one of our (ahem) rather heated discussions, he said to me indignantly, "You want me to *change!*" To which I responded with some amazement, "Are you trying to tell me you never want to change *anything* about yourself? Ever? You want to be exactly the person you are now for the rest of your life?"

I happened to see Bubba a couple of years ago when he returned to town for his father's funeral. It had been about twenty-five years since I'd seen him, and he was, in fact, *exactly* the same person he'd been when I'd known him. The sad thing was that he was even more unhappy, and he *knew* that this was because he hadn't been willing to make any changes in himself—and even so, he *still* wasn't planning to change.

My own journey, on the other hand, has been filled with change, some of it quite drastic. At the point when Bubba and I were together, I was also truly miserable and had been for most of my life. But I finally got sick of being depressed and unhappy (and I got literally sick, which turned out to be a great motivator) and decided that I was going to do whatever it took to change my negative attitude into something more positive.

It took years and some good help, and—as with most things—it is still a work in progress. But these days I can honestly say that I am generally happy and content—a positive, upbeat, perky person. (Okay, that perky part is a lie. But the rest is true.) This doesn't mean that I am perfect—hell no—or that there isn't plenty of work still to be done or that I don't have bad days or get discouraged like everyone else. What it does mean is that change is not only possible, it is *necessary* if we are going to achieve the goal that most of us share: to become the best Witch and human being that we can be.

You can choose to be a Bubba and cling to your unhappiness or your bad habits because they are what you know and you are comfortable with them, no matter how miserable they make you and the people around you.

Or you can choose to work toward positive change as you walk along the path of the everyday Witch. Because there can be no growth without change, and Pagans are all about growth.

So what does any of this have to do with Witchcraft and nature, you ask? Well, I'll tell you. There are a lot of lessons to be learned from watching the natural world and trying to go with its energetic flow. The story about how becoming a Pagan cured my winter blues is just one example. The biggest point of that example was to show how it is a lot easier to move *with* those energies than it is to try working *against* them.

Think of it like this: when you walk in and out of the ocean, it is a lot easier to come in as the waves come in and go out as the waves go out. If you try to force yourself through the waves as they are moving in the opposite direction, it takes much more energy to take those steps.

Life is much like that ocean. If you can figure out which way the waves of the universe are flowing at any given time, you will have to expend a lot less energy of your own to get much larger results. And that's where the Wheel of the Year and the lunar cycle come in.

The Wheel of the Year: Energy and Endeavor

The Wheel of the Year follows the natural cycle of birth, growth, death, and rebirth. The simplest example of this would be a flower, which comes up through the earth, blooms, goes back to the earth, and plants its seeds to be born again the next spring. As Pagans, we believe that we, too, follow this cycle: we are born, live our lives, die, and then are reincarnated to do it all over again.

Sometimes, as with the flower, the entire cycle goes by quite rapidly. Other times it is a slow, ponderous process, like the oak tree that can take hundreds of years to reach its full growth and then begin to die off, piece by piece. Personal change can be like that, too. Sometimes it happens quickly (you wake up one morning and say, "That's it—this is my last cigarette!" and you quit, just like that). Sometimes progress is so slow that you can't even see it happening if you watch, and it is only when you turn and look back at where you came from that you can see how far you've come.

There's no right or wrong way to create positive change in your life, but you might make it easier on yourself if you follow the energy of the yearly cycle of the Wheel. Each season has its own rhythm and its own energetic predisposition. If you can focus on working on problems and issues that go along with those preestablished patterns, you may find the process will go easier and faster.

Spring

Spring is the time for birth or rebirth. This is the best time of the year to start new projects, focus your goals for the year, and plant the seeds for what you want to achieve. Don't expect rapid movement, though, since things have to get going at their own pace (which could be fast, since many plants in the spring seem to just appear from nowhere, but could also be slow, like a tulip poking its head gradually out of the ground).

Summer

Summer is when the earth's energy is at its most abundant. This is the time to really push ahead with whatever you're working on. Growth is faster now, and changes may be more powerful (and therefore more frightening, sometimes, but hang in there). Tap into the energy of the sun and the light to shine clarity into murky situations, and don't be afraid to go charging ahead if it feels right to do so.

Fall

Things are starting to slow down now. This is when you harvest what you've achieved, and check back in with your goals to see which ones you didn't make as much progress with as you would have liked to. Fall is also a time to reassess; if you didn't manage to do what you wanted, try to figure out what it was that stood in your way. Just as the Oak King sacrifices himself for the good of the land, sometimes we have to figure out which things don't work for us anymore and clear them away so that growth can happen in their place. Are there people who aren't a positive force in your life? Does your job suck your soul out without giving you much in return? Are you too busy making excuses to accomplish the work you need to be doing? Now is the time to take a good long look at what you didn't accomplish, and figure out what you can change to make things different the next time around. But it is also the time to celebrate the goals you did achieve, and pat yourself on the back for a job well done.

Winter

Now the pace of the natural world slows down; some things die entirely and some merely lie dormant, waiting for the return of the warmth and the light. This is the time to turn inward, to be quiet, and to let your spirit renew itself after a long year of striving. Most of us still have to go to work and clean the house and keep ourselves and our families fed. But there are ways to slow down, even in the midst of the busy world around us. Turn off the TV and the computer more often and read a book, meditate, have game night with the kids, take a bath, go to bed earlier. Allow yourself to be a little less "go go go" and a little more "ahhh." You can plot and plan and dream about the year ahead, but winter tends not to be the best time to start new things. The spring will come again soon enough, and the entire cycle will begin again.

Of course, this is all general. Life rarely follows the rules, and if you are offered the perfect new job in the middle of the winter or need to start a new project in the fall, by all means do so. This is more of a general guide to making your own optional choices at the time that is most likely to work in your favor.

The Lunar Cycle: Waxing and Waning

Like the Wheel of the Year, the cycle of the ever-changing moon can affect the energy around us. The lunar cycle is divided into two halves, waxing and waning, with the full moon standing in the middle. The full moon is arguably the most powerful night in the month, and many Witches choose to do their most potent and important magickal work then. But it can also be useful to tap into the particular flow of the rest of the month in order to achieve your desires and goals.

Full Moon

For many Pagans, the moon is a symbol of the Goddess, and the night of the full moon is a time of worship and appreciation, as well as a good time to take five minutes to address whatever issues are most important in your life that month.

Here are a few five-minute rituals that work well on the night of the full moon:

STAND OUTSIDE UNDER THE MOON OR LOOK AT IT OUT A WINDOW—Close your eyes and feel yourself bathed in its light. Feel the power of the moon pulling at your soul. If you want, chant or even howl. Gather up that light and power and pull it into your core to help recharge you for the coming month.

DANCE IN THE MOONLIGHT—Take five minutes and give yourself up to joy. Celebrate the Goddess and the deity inside you. You can put on drumming or some kind of Pagan music or just dance to the music inside your own soul. Don't worry about what anyone will think or how you look. Just be in the moment and give yourself permission to dance.

SAY A SPELL—Whatever you need, now is a good time to work on it. For a variety of spells to deal with practical everyday issues, check out my book *Everyday Witch A to Z Spellbook*, *Encyclopedia of 500 Spells* by Judika Illes, or *Spells for Tough Times* by Kerri Conner.

Waning Moon

The waning half of the moon's cycle starts as soon as the full moon begins to grow smaller and lasts through to the dark moon (when the moon isn't visible at all). The waning moon is best used for any magickal work that has to do with *decrease*. So if you want to get rid of something or have less of something, you might want to work on that during the waning moon.

A few five-minute rituals for the waning moon include:

DECREASING VISUALIZATION—Light a small candle; a tiny beeswax candle will dwindle rapidly or you can use a birthday candle. Write the thing you want to decrease on a piece of paper and put it under the candle or simply fix it in your mind. As you watch the candle growing smaller and smaller, visualize your issue (debt, weight, illness, stress, etc.) getting smaller too.

DRINK IT DOWN—Pour some water into a clear glass or goblet. Put both hands around it and lift it up, saying something like: "This is _____, which I wish to decrease in my life." Drink the water sip by sip, repeating the sentence until the water is gone, and then say, "So mote it be."

RIBBON RITUAL—For a quick ritual that can be done in a minute or two every day for the duration of the waning moon, write the thing you wish to reduce or get rid of on a piece of ribbon. Then snip off a small piece every night, timing it so that the last piece is gone by the next full moon.

Waxing Moon

The waxing moon is when the moon begins to grow larger in the sky again, starting the day after the dark moon, and this time is best used for any magickal work to do with *increase*. So if you want more of something—health, money, love, or whatever—you can tap into the natural energy for increase that is available at this time.

Here are a few five-minute rituals that tap into the natural energies of the waxing moon:

STONE RITUAL—Gather a small bunch of stones, preferably ones that have flat sides or uneven edges so they will pile together without falling. Each night of the waxing moon, take a moment to think of what it is you want to increase in your life and add a stone to your pile until you have a little cairn by the end of the two weeks.

SALT RITUAL—You can do the same thing with salt if you don't have stones. Put some salt (preferably sea salt or salt you have consecrated for magickal work) into a container with a spout. Pour the salt into a small bowl, watching each tiny piece adding to the whole and getting larger and larger. Visualize whatever you want to increase growing slowly but surely, bit by bit through your efforts. (This can be done on one night or over many.)

GROWTH SPELL—Plant a fast-growing seed or bulb at the beginning of the waxing time (cat grass works well for this, and then you can share it with your feline pal, should you have one; radishes, carrots, peas, or beans often poke their heads up pretty rapidly, as do zinnias, marigolds, cosmos, and sunflowers). Place a piece of paper under or in the dirt you are using with the specifics of what you want to grow. Take a couple of minutes every day to put your energy into the seed, sending energy for growth into your wish as well.

Connecting with the Elements: Earth, Air, Fire, and Water

We use the four elements—earth, air, fire, and water—in many of our rituals. But how much time and attention do we pay them outside of sacred space? Usually, not a lot. In truth, I suspect we tend to take them for granted because they are all around us: the rain falls from the sky and the water comes out of the faucet, fire warms us and lights our candles, we breathe the air without thinking about it, and our feet tread the earth every day.

But as Witches, earth, air, fire, and water are so much more than that; in fact, they are key components to our spiritual practice. So here are some fast, easy, inexpensive, and fun ways to work on your connections to the elements.

Earth

One of the great things about the element of earth is that it is *everywhere.* There are places without abundant water and times when you don't want to have a fire, but you don't have to look far to find earth, which is literally under your feet. (If you live in a high-rise apartment, it may be *far* under your feet, but I guarantee you it is down there somewhere.) It is in the plants and trees and rocks. It is even in your kitchen in the form of salt, which many people use to stand for the earth element during rituals.

Earth is the element usually associated with the north, midnight, and winter. Its colors are most commonly brown, green, black, and sometimes gold. It rules the physical body, nature, money, trees and plants, rocks and crystals, animals, and death. The three zodiac signs associated with earth are Taurus, Virgo, and Capricorn.

Ironically, in the modern world, this may be the element that many people are least in touch with, spiritually speaking. But I have a number of easy and inexpensive options to fix that. Just pick one or two and try them out, and remember that when you are connecting with earth, you are also connecting with the Earth—Mother Gaia. That can only be a good thing.

GROUND AND CENTER

Many rituals tell you to "ground and center" as a starting point; unfortunately, hardly anyone explains what that means or how to do it, despite its importance to a Witchcraft practice. It is simple and easy, and a great way to deepen your connection to the earth element. The goal of "ground and center" is to find your own internal center (most people perceive that as being around their navel) and to root it strongly in preparation for either meditation or magickal work.

The best way to do this is to go outside and sit or stand directly on the ground. If you're inside, then sit or stand on the floor (some people like to take their shoes off, but you don't have to). For those who can't stand or find sitting on the floor uncomfortable, it is fine to sit in a chair with your feet flat on the floor.

Close your eyes and take a few slow, deep breaths. Feel the ground beneath you. (If you are inside, simply sense the ground underneath whatever floor you are on.) Feel the strength of the earth, how solid and dependable it is, and visualize a root forming at the base of your spine or coming out your feet and reaching down into the earth. Visualize that root spreading out and going deeper until you are firmly rooted in the ground. Draw some of that strength up into you. If you like, you can also reach up into the sky above, toward the light.

That is grounding and centering, and it is probably the most potent way to connect with the earth. If you want to take it one step further, you can go out and lie on the ground, and feel yourself becoming one with the land beneath you. When you're done, simply bring your consciousness back to where you began.

PLAYING IN THE DIRT

Another great way to connect with the element of earth is to literally play with it. I do that in my garden all the time, but if you have neither the space nor the inclination to take on anything that large, all you need is a small pot, some soil, a small container of water, and a few seeds or a bulb.

Obviously, people plant things all the time, so the key to taking this activity one step further is to be really aware and focused, concentrating not just on the task but also on making this all-important connection. Gather your tools (if you're doing something small inside, a spoon will do, or even the tip of your athame). You can plant anything you want, but this exercise will be even more meaningful if you plant some herb seeds and then use them in your rituals after they're grown. But you can easily plant something that will grow into a beautiful flower, such as a crocus, if that makes you happier.

Make sure that the soil you are using is good and healthy—organic is best, of course, but either way it should be a lovely brown color and smell earthy and good. If you're not going to be outside, place everything on your altar (protecting the surface with a cloth) or kitchen counter so that everything you need is within reach.

Pick up the soil and hold some of it in your hands. Crumble it between your fingers and hold it up to your nose. Look at it closely; see the variations in color and texture, the tiny stones or bits of bark or tree or whatever else might be in it. If you're in a garden, you may see an earthworm (great helpers in the garden!) or a bug or two. Be sure to thank them for the work they do. Plunge your hands into the soil or hold it in your palm. Close your eyes and feel the potential for growth inside it. When you're ready, put the seeds into the soil and water them gently and with reverence. Then send a little bit of growing energy and blessing into the seeds and the soil. Don't forget to check on your plant later to see what the earth has achieved!

A CLAY GOD/DESS IN YOUR OWN IMAGE

Witches believe that the gods exist outside of us and inside us at the same time. We are each a piece of Goddess/God. Blue Moon Circle once did a really fun magickal project using clay: we each made a Goddess figure that was also a representation of ourselves. One of the things that made it so much fun was how different each person's image ended up being. There were some very simple goddesses, some with elaborate long hair and abundant bosoms decorated with beads and shells and leaves, and one person even made her figurine in the shape of a decorated egg to represent the potential she felt inside herself.

This craft is an opportunity to connect not only with earth, but with God/dess and with self. If you do it in a group, you will probably enjoy a certain amount of mirth along with your reverence; done alone, it can be a deep and spiritual experience.

Clay can be found at craft stores, the craft sections of some larger stores, and online. If you are lucky enough to live in an area where clay occurs naturally, you can just go outside and scoop some up. Just be sure that you are using true clay and not artificial or polymer clay, which is made from plastic; that would completely defeat the purpose. You can also use any decorations you want, including small rocks or beads, seeds, dried flowers such as rose petals or calendula, acorns, shells, etc.

If you want, you can do this inside a sacred circle, or you can simply sit outside or at the kitchen table. Gather all your supplies and a few tools; toothpicks or the tip of your athame work well for drawing on your clay. If possible, it is nice to do this on the night of the full moon.

Pull off a chunk of clay and hold it, feeling it growing more malleable as you work it with the heat of your hands. If you need to, you can add a few drops of water. Think about the fact that your body and this clay are made of many of the same elements, and that the Goddess is in the clay just as she is in you. Mold the clay into whatever shape feels right to you, and decorate it however you please. If you want to add a more magickal element, you can place your wishes or dreams into your God/dess figure on a slip of paper (men may want to make a god figure; you can choose either or both). Once it is done, place it on your altar or someplace safe. Eventually, you may wish to bury it outside, returning it to Mother Earth.

If you don't feel like making a statue or image, try making your own set of rune stones instead. My first group was led by a woman who happened to be a potter, so we used regular clay that she later fired in her kiln. But you can also buy clay that either dries without firing or can be baked in a regular oven.

Making rune stones is simple. Find a chart or book that shows you all the rune symbols (my favorite is A Practical Guide to the Runes: Their Uses in Divination and Magick by Lisa Peschel). Take small pieces of clay and shape them into twenty-five small oval or rectangular tiles of approximately the same size and shape. Scratch a rune sign into each one except the last, which is left empty. If you want, you can decorate the other side with whatever designs you like or you can leave them blank. I put my thumbprint into each one to make it more "mine."

Once they are done and dry (and fired if you're going to do that), you can paint them. I left mine plain because I like the texture and look of the simple clay; it made me feel connected somehow to the ancient Pagans who made such things long ago that looked and felt much the same. You can also bless and consecrate them, then store them in either a nice drawstring bag or a special box. When you use them, don't forget to thank the element of earth for its help.

EASY STONE DIVINATION

A friend of mine taught me this really simple divination technique, which is done outside. Pick an area where there are a number of rocks and stones (we used my driveway, which tells you something about my driveway). Close your eyes and take a few deep breaths, asking the gods for guidance. Fix a question in your mind to which you would like an answer. Then walk backward (carefully) until you feel like you have reached the right spot. Pick up the rock closest to you. Look at it carefully to see if you can make out any signs or symbols.

This sounds a little crazy, I know, but when I did it, soon after moving in, I could see two clear pictures in the indentations on the rock: the outlines of a house and a heart. That rock is still sitting on one of my altars. Try it—you never know.

MAKING THE CONNECTION

These are just a few examples of how to connect with this strong, rooted element. Don't forget that when you feel in need of grounding or something solid to keep you focused when the world around you seems hectic and out of control, you need look no further than the earth under your feet. Or, of course, you can go outside and hug a tree. That works too (and I think they like it).

Air

Although not everyone follows the same exact correspondences, air is usually associated with the direction east, with communication and thought, and with the spring. It is often represented by the color yellow and can be symbolized on the altar by a feather or incense. Air is associated with the zodiac signs of Gemini, Aquarius, and Libra.

Those are the basics—but how can we make a deeper connection (without spending money on fancy decorations or tools)? Luckily, air is the "cheapest" of all the elements, since it is everywhere around us. All we have to do is make a little effort and figure out how to connect with something invisible and untouchable...

Here are a few suggestions for you to try. Hopefully one or more of them will resonate with your own personal practice.

JUST BREATHE

Air exists outside of us, but we take it in with every breath. One of the simplest ways to form a deeper association with the element of air is to take some time to breathe mindfully. You can do this while you are taking a walk or sitting by the water (should you be fortunate enough to have a body of water to sit beside) or even in your car waiting for your kid to be done with baseball practice. But if you want something a little more focused, here is a simple exercise that anyone can do:

Sit comfortably, either inside or outside. Close your eyes. Breathe in and out slowly, paying attention to the way the air feels in your nostrils, your throat, and your lungs. Feel the presence of the air as it surrounds you. If there is a breeze, feel its caress against your skin. Think about the fact that the air is everywhere around you like a comforting blanket, weightless and invisible but always there, always dependable, like an old friend. It has been with you since the first breath you took as a baby, and it will be with you until the last breath you take on the day you die. Breathe deeply, taking the air inside you. A moment ago it was outside you, separate from you, and now it is a part of you. Feel that connection, and feel the way it connects you, in turn, with the rest of the world. Breathe in and out, slowly and deeply, and feel yourself *becoming* air.

INVOCATIONS AND INCANTATIONS

If you think about it, the spoken word is a way of taking air and transforming it into sound. How magickal is that? Without air, there would be no speech. Seriously, just try it. Start reading this out loud and see how far you get without taking a new breath; it won't be very far. No wonder air is the element associated with communication.

So while you might light a candle or a bonfire to celebrate the element of fire, one of the easiest (and free!) ways to celebrate air is with the power of the spoken word. Try doing the meditation above and then writing a poem, invocation, or spell to show your appreciation for this all-important element. (You don't have to do the air practice first, of course, but by deepening your connection first, you will really be in the zone when you come up with your written piece.)

You don't have to be a great writer to do this. For that matter, you don't have to write it down at all, since our goal here is to come up with the spoken word. You can always just spontaneously speak from the heart. But if you are more comfortable having something prepared or if you want to play around with it to get it just right, then you can certainly write it out.

Your poem or invocation doesn't have to rhyme, although it might. You can use it as an invocation when you call the quarters or you can just use it this once to complete this exercise. Here is a simple example, although what you come up with may be very different. (You can also just say this one out loud if you can't come up with something yourself.)

> Element of air
> Gentle as the breeze
> Powerful as the hurricane
> You carry our songs through the sky
> To the God and Goddess above
> Through you our drumbeats resonate
> Our heartbeats echo
> And the laughter of children rings
> You give us life
> And so we thank you
> Element of air

Okay, now you do one! And don't forget to read it out loud, using your breath to carry your message to the spirits of the air.

If you are not a "spoken word" kind of person, there are lots of other methods you can utilize to communicate with the powers of air. As the invocation above says, you can sing, drum, or do anything else that causes vibrations in the air around you. Just make sure they're joyful and filled with gratitude and appreciation.

CREATE AN ALTAR

Many of us have altars that contain a little something that represents each of the elements. But you can also create an altar that is dedicated to a particular god, goddess, or element. For instance, as a Taurus, I am very earth-oriented and am more likely to have an earth-centric altar. But if you are an airy type—a Gemini, Aquarius, or Libra—you may want to put together an altar to the element of air. (Or do one for each element and place them in the appropriate corners of the room.)

You might start with an altar cloth in one of the colors associated with air: white, yellow, pale blue, or pale gray. If you are crafty, you can embroider or quilt or paint an air scene on the cloth—maybe something with clouds and birds. (You don't need to spend a lot of money on a fancy cloth done by someone else; it's better to do something that comes from the heart!) If possible, the altar should face east, but it doesn't matter if you can't make that work.

An air altar will have representations of various things associated with the element such as the god Mercury, for instance, or a feather, a bell (to represent sound), a sage smudge stick, or incense. If you don't like incense, you can substitute an oil diffuser, since the scent of the oil will still be carried upward into the air. Scents usually associated with air include lemon, lavender, and rosemary. Since air is the realm of the intellect, you could add a book—even your Book of Shadows.

Then light a yellow candle and, if you like, recite your incantation, a poem, or the invocation above. Try standing at your air altar at dawn, especially in the spring. (You may want to put up an air altar in the spring, then replace it with a fire altar in the summer, a water altar in the fall, and an earth altar in the winter.)

AIR IN ALL ITS GUISES

Air is one of the most changeable of all the elements. Sometimes it is calm and quiet; other times, raging and full of fury. Instead of taking these various guises for granted, try going outside in all weather and at all times of day, making a mindful connection with all the different faces of this ever-present element.

Wake up early and greet the dawn, breathing in the clean, clear air of a new day. Go out after a storm and smell the crisp ozone that lingers even after the rain is gone. How is the air different in the spring, the summer, the fall, or on a cool winter's evening? Listen to the birds singing their greetings, and recite your own with mindful appreciation. Think about the ways that air may mirror your own moods or vice versa!

CONNECTION IS WHAT IT IS ALL ABOUT

To me, connection is at the core of a Pagan practice and living a magickal life. Connecting with the elements is just one way to walk that path, which includes connecting with self, with others, and with deity. Because we take in air every time we breathe, it is the easiest element to connect with. Be sure to remember that every time you use air to say those three magickal words I *love you*.

Fire

I have a confession to make: my coven and I have a few issues with fire. Candles don't stay lit, it takes thirty-seven matches to get the bonfire going, and then it starts raining and puts the fire out. It happens so often, we jokingly call ourselves "The Fire-Impaired Witches." I don't know why this is, exactly, but it doesn't in any way interfere with our love of this particular element; despite our challenges, we integrate it in our practice as much as possible. After all, we've only been doing this work together for eight or so years…we have to get good at it eventually!

Fire is the element associated with the south, which makes sense when you think about which parts of the country and the world are the hottest. In the same way, it is also associated with noon and summer. Fire rules creativity, passion, energy, courage, healing, and the blood. It is usually represented by bright and energetic colors such as red, orange, and gold, and it is associated with the zodiac signs Sagittarius, Leo, and Aries.

Those are the basics (which, as always, each Witch will alter to suit her own practice and instincts)—but how do we go from lists of correspondences to actually using and connecting with the element of fire? Here are a few suggestions.

LET THE LIGHT SHINE OUT

One of the most commonly used fire tools is the candle. Many of us use candles at every quarter (with red for south and the element of fire), but even when we use other items to symbolize air (such as a feather), water (a shell, for instance, or a cup of water), and earth (a rock or a crystal), a candle is almost always the favorite choice to represent fire. With its light that shines in the darkest night and the warmth of the Goddess/God's love, it represents hope.

Candles have been around since the dawn of civilization, used in drafty castles and threadbare cottages alike. Originally, most candles were made from tallow (derived from the fat of sheep and cows) or beeswax (which was usually reserved for the wealthy or the church). These days the majority of candles are made from paraffin wax (a petroleum byproduct) and sometimes soy.

Thankfully, since most Pagans use candles for rituals, prayer, and ceremony, this is one tool that is reasonably inexpensive. Candles come in a remarkable variety with various scents and colors, and they can be bought pre-blessed and consecrated from numerous magickal supply shops. But if you are trying to find a way to connect with the element of fire, I strongly recommend making (or creating) your own.

Making candles is fairly simple, and you can find both supplies and instructions online or at a local craft store. Just remember to be careful when melting wax (it gets HOT and can burn your skin or even catch on fire if you're not careful—and that is not how we want to make this all-important connection, is it?). You may want to experiment a little bit before making your special magickal version.

So how is making a magickal candle different from making any other kind of candle at home? Focus and intent, of course.

While you're making your candle, be sure to keep your intent in mind. Are you making a candle for prosperity magick? To begin with, you may want to add some green candle coloring and a few drops of essential oil from one or more of the herbs associated with prosperity. (If you want to be even cheaper, you can use a crayon in the color you desire or add the tag-end of an almost-used-up older candle.)

But more than that, as you pour your wax or dip your candle (depending on the technique you are using), focus on what you wish to achieve. If your purpose is connecting with the element of fire, keep that in mind, too.

If you don't want to bother with the fuss and muss of making a candle from scratch, you can buy one and add your own special touches to it, thereby putting a bit of your own magick into a premade tool. I like to etch magickal symbols and runes onto the sides of "ordinary" candles and anoint them with magickal oils. When Blue Moon Circle is doing a ritual that involves candle magick, we usually spend some time during the ritual doing this and talking about our goals before saying the spell and lighting the candles together. When you add these extra steps, candle magick can be very powerful indeed—all set into motion when you add fire.

To connect more deeply with the element of fire through candles, try this simple ritual:

Take a candle (either one you made yourself or one you made more magickal through the steps I talked about above) and place it in a fire-safe container or holder. Sit in a darkened room with the candle in front of you; it is especially nice if you can do this on the night of the full moon so that the only other light in the room comes from the moon's magickal glow. Light a match, being mindful of the snap of fire as it bursts into flame and the smell of the sulfur. Hold the match to the wick and feel the connection as the flame leaps from one to the other. Blow out the match and see how the fire lives on in its new host, the candle. Carefully put your hand over the candle and lower it until you can feel the heat, first as a vague warmth, then hotter. Careful—don't burn yourself! Fire is a useful tool, but never forget that if used carelessly, fire can burn down houses or even entire forests. Think about your admiration and respect for this powerful element. Then sit for a while and admire it before thanking fire for all it does and blowing out the candle.

BURN, BABY, BURN

There is a reason why many of the old pictures of Witches show them dancing (naked or not) around a bonfire. Fire is an indispensable part of ritual, whether it is used for heating up a cauldron full of magickal potions or simply sending sparks out into the universe to carry our intentions up to the gods. If you live in a place that allows for the use of a bonfire, I highly recommend adding this fire element to your rites.

One of my favorite things to do with a bonfire is to harness the fire to burn away those things I no longer need. I often perform rituals that involve writing something on a slip of paper (or at harvest season on a corn-husk) and throwing it into the fire to burn clean. Bonfires are also great for tossing dried herbs into: lavender for love and healing, for instance, or rosemary for remembrance or sage for purification.

And, like the Witches of old, bonfires *are* great to dance around. Beltane is traditionally celebrated by leaping the Beltane bonfire, a way of bringing in luck. (Don't do this if you are accident prone or wearing long, flammable garments!) But bonfires don't have to be saved for special occasions, and there is no better way to get in touch with your inner Witch and all the Pagans that walked this path before you than to dance around a bonfire—if possible, to the beat of a wild drum. Look—the flames are dancing with you! (And while most of us can't do a bonfire on an everyday basis, it is fine to substitute a candle and dance around that.)

NONFLAMMABLE FLAME

Not everyone is lucky enough to have a fire pit in their backyard or even to live in a place that allows open flames of any kind. Dorm rooms, for instance, often have rules against lighting any kind of fire, and if you are at a Pagan conference that is held at a hotel, in all likelihood there will be no candles allowed there either. Or you want to have a bonfire for your ritual, but you live in an apartment. What's a Witch to do?

There are a few alternatives to the traditional tools that will still allow you to bring the element of fire into your ritual. For instance, they make small battery-operated lights that look like flickering candles. Or if you want to simulate a bonfire but you're stuck inside, you can make a small contained fire using Epsom salts and rubbing alcohol in a fire-safe container. (This will still get hot, so be careful. However, it doesn't give off smoke like a real bonfire.) One of my favorite faux fire alternatives is a cauldron with paper flames and LED lights that flicker. A battery makes the fake flames move, so it simulates the feel of a bonfire. It's not a perfect solution, but if you can't have the real thing, it isn't bad. And they're reasonably cheap: between twenty and thirty dollars for a tabletop version.

FIRE ON THE ALTAR

If you want to build a fire altar—either to honor the element at any time or to celebrate it during one of the fire festivals like Beltane or for the duration of the summer season—there are a few inexpensive and easy ways to go about it.

You can start with an altar cloth in red, orange, gold, or a combination of the three. Try using a simple red tablecloth or a large napkin (depending on the size of your altar); you can probably find one at a dollar store, Goodwill, or at a yard sale, or you can make your own from a piece of fabric. Using gold fabric paint, you can draw on any symbols you like: a flame, the sun, a lightning bolt, or something along those lines. You can also add the names of any gods or goddesses who have fire in their powers, such as Hephaestus or Hestia, who was the goddess of the hearth fire. You might want to add Prometheus, who brought the gift of fire to humankind. There are fire deities in almost every culture, so no matter what path you follow, you will find some god or goddess who rules over the power of this element.

Then you can place symbols of fire on the altar, including candles, charcoal, various types of wood to form a mini bonfire (this is just for show, not to burn), a chunk of obsidian (since it is a stone that is formed in the fire of a volcano), a small iron cauldron, or anything else that speaks of fire to you.

COOKING UP SOME MAGICK

If you want to make a magickal connection with fire, cook over an open flame. Barbeques are perfect for this, but even a gas stove will do. Try having a fire-themed cook out, with spicy food and maybe a chocolate lava cake for dessert.

In truth, any form of cooking that involves heat can be a celebration of fire. As you stir the pot upon the stove, give thanks for the element that allows us to cook delicious feasts for ourselves and our families.

HERE COMES THE SUN

The biggest symbol of fire is the sun, without which life wouldn't exist on our planet. For a fast and easy way to celebrate the sun, simply take five minutes to sit in a patch of sunlight, soaking up its warmth and light. If you're lucky you can do this sitting on a beach, where you can also connect with water, earth, and air at the same time. But even if you are only in your own backyard or even curled up in the middle of your bed, you can feel the power and heat of fire in its powerful rays. While you're sitting in the sun, you may want to do a brief meditation on fire's traits of passion and energy, looking within to find those things inside yourself and fan the embers into stronger flames to motivate you through the rest of your day.

MAKING THE CONNECTION

It doesn't really matter whether you dance around a bonfire or light a candle or even just close your eyes and feel the passion we all hold at our core. What's important is that you take a moment during ritual to greet the element of fire and remember to thank it for all the wonderful gifts it brings to our lives. After all, without fire, there would be no cooking—and we Pagans love our feasts! So throw something into the cauldron for yourself and a few friends, and light a candle in gratitude for the wonderful power of fire.

Water

In one form or another, water is everywhere. In many ways it can be the most mutable element of them all, taking the outward appearance of a liquid, a solid (snow or ice), or even something in between (mist or fog). Water is a wonderful tool for any magickal work that involves change or requires flexibility, and it can be found all around us.

The element of water is connected in most modern Witchcraft practices with the west, twilight, and autumn. It is also associated with the emotions (which makes sense, since what could be more changeable?), intuition, fertility, and cleansing. The colors of water are those you would expect if you have ever looked into a pond or stood by the ocean's shore: blues, blue-green, and gray, primarily, with the addition of white in some instances. The zodiac water signs are Cancer, Scorpio, and Pisces (the fish).

Water is as easy to come by as turning on the tap, but for magickal uses, some people prefer to use water from a more natural source, including wells and springs, ponds and rivers, and the ocean. If you don't have access to any of those, you can always put out a container to catch rainwater or collect snow if it is winter. Of course, in a pinch, turning on the faucet will certainly work too.

Working with the element of water can be as simple as taking a bath or as complicated as a formal tea ceremony. Here are a few simple suggestions for integrating this most agreeable of elements in to your regular magickal practices.

CLEANSING AND CLEARING

The most basic use of water is as an aid to cleansing or clearing—whether you are talking about yourself, your tools, or even a space (whether living space or a magickal circle). But doing so isn't quite as simple as stepping into the shower or taking a walk in the rain. Remember that intent matters in magick. So if you need to clean a crystal, for instance, you don't want to just plunk it in a bowl of water. You're not trying to clear only the surface of gunk, after all, but also the aura, or energy, of the stone. For that you need a little more effort.

Some Witches keep a supply of blessed and consecrated water around for use in rituals, which isn't a bad idea. It is simple enough to make: gather some rainwater, spring water, or whatever you want to use (tap water will do if you don't have anything else). Place the water on your altar or out under the full moon; a windowsill will do if you can't leave it outside. It is nice to use a special container—a pitcher, bowl, or decorated jar—that is saved for only this use. Ask the gods or your spiritual powers/guides to bless the water for magickal use. If you like, you can sprinkle a little sea salt in it, waft a sage wand over it, or even leave a crystal in the water overnight.

To cleanse a magickal tool, you will first want to get the most pure water you have available to you or use a preconsecrated magickal water such as that described above. If the tool is something that won't be harmed by water, such as a stone or crystal, then you can immerse it in a bowl. It can be placed on your altar or in the light of a full moon with the intention of clearing and cleansing it of any negative or unwanted energy. NOTE: it is a good idea to cleanse all new tools, especially if you are uncertain about their source. A crystal that spent months sitting in a shop, for instance, might have picked up all sorts of scattered energy.

If the tool can't be placed directly in the water (like an athame or a wooden wand), you can place a cloth underneath the item and then sprinkle water over it, saying something along the lines of this:

Cleanse and clear this magickal tool, and leave it pure of energy
and ready for positive work. So mote it be.

Be sure to dry off the tool afterward.

If you need to cleanse yourself, you can do something as simple as placing a bowl of water on your altar (if you have one) or on a table. Close your eyes and focus on the beneficial cleansing properties of the water and your intent to clear away negativity or bad feelings. Then dip your fingertips or your entire hands into the water and sprinkle a little over your head and dab it onto your third eye (in the middle of your forehead), your eyelids, your lips, your heart, your core (under your belly button), and anywhere else that feels like it needs to be purified. Then dip your hands one more time and wipe them off on a towel, visualizing your energy field shining brightly.

For a more intense cleaning, you can take a bath (with or without the addition of salt, cleansing herbs, or essential oils), a shower, or go for a walk in the rain. Just remember to focus on your intent to let the water wash away anything you no longer want or need.

THE POWER OF PERSISTENCE

Water may seem soft and mild, but it can be a truly powerful force. A tsunami, after all, is just water—lots and lots of really powerful water. Less obvious but just as important is the ability of water to wear away at things over time. The Grand Canyon, for instance, was slowly created over many, many years by the flow of water. If you need help in finding your own inner strength to persist in the face of long odds, you might want to consider doing some water magick.

Try this simple ritual:

Write your goal on a piece of paper. Focus all your intent on your determination to keep working toward that goal no matter how long it takes—day after day, one foot after the other. Then place a small pile of sand (or salt) in a bowl and get a small pitcher filled with water. You can even use an eyedropper if you happen to have one around.

Place the piece of paper with your goal on it underneath the sand or salt, and very slowly add the water one small drop at a time. With each drop, say:

Like the water, I will persist. Like the water, I will wear away
all that stands between me and my goal.

(You can specify your goal, such as "between me and achieving the goal of owning my own home" or whatever it is.)

When the water has washed away enough sand to reveal the paper with your goal on it, say, "So mote it be, and so it is." Repeat whenever you feel like you need the boost.

INTERCONNECTION

One of the aspects of water I love the most is the way it is connected to the rest of the world; the raindrop that falls in my garden might once have lived as a drop of water in the ocean. We are all made of water—adults can be up to 60 percent water, and babies are even more. I like to think that all that water connects us both to the earth and each other. Every time we drink a glass of water or take a shower or stand in the rain, we are also walking in the ocean. The water that flows through my body is just like the water that flows through yours, no matter where we live, what color we are, or what our sexuality, religious practices, or age is. We are all water.

If you are feeling the need to connect with people or the planet, try this simple meditation:

Place a glass of water where you can reach it. Sit comfortably and take a sip. Close your eyes and feel the water sliding down your throat. Visualize the molecules that make up the water spreading out to nourish the cells of your body until you are glowing with health and vitality. Now visualize the invisible moisture in the air around you; you can't see it, but it is always there. Feel the connection between the water you just swallowed—now a part of your entire body—and the water in the air. Send your awareness out on that moisture, sensing how it connects you to the people around you, the people farther away, the rain-filled clouds far above you, and the water flowing deep underground. Spreading your awareness out further, feel the rivers and the fish swimming in them; feel the oceans and all the creatures that call the sea home. Rising up, view the earth from above and see all the places where water is bringing life. Embrace this world and feel yourself a part of it, then slowly come back to awareness of your own body. Open your eyes and take another sip of water. Ah...

FLEXIBILITY AND GOING WITH THE FLOW

One of the toughest skills to master is the ability to take life's ups and downs in stride. We all want to handle the tough stuff with grace and dignity, but it can be hard to go with the flow.

Water can teach us a lot about being flexible. It changes shape and texture depending on the circumstances. A wide river may narrow until it becomes a skinny creek and then expand to become a pond. It can freeze and then thaw and then turn into tiny, delicate snowflakes (or, if you live in ° New York and some other places, giant pieces of hail as big as golf balls). It can turn into a fog so thick you can't see through it or make a lake so smooth and still you can see yourself in it like a mirror. If only we could all be as flexible as water!

When you need to work on your ability to go with the flow of life's circumstances, try this easy spell. All you need is some water and a few glasses or clear containers of different sizes and shapes. If you can do this outside under a full moon with the light shining on the water, that's great. Otherwise, just stand in front of your altar or a table.

Start with the water in one container, and hold the container up before your eyes. See the way the water fits inside the glass. Then pour it carefully into another container and see it change to fit the shape of its new home. Repeat this a few times, really paying attention to the way the water shifts and changes effortlessly. It loses nothing from the change; it is still the same water.

Hold the water up to the sky and say:

> Like the water, I will go with the flow of life. I will change when
> change is needed; I will shift with grace. I will be flexible and calm.
> I am the water; I go with the flow.

If you are outside, you can pour the water on the ground to nourish the soil. Otherwise you can drink it or even water your plants with it. You're flexible—you'll think of something!

POWER WATER

You can buy all sorts of expensive fancy waters that will supposedly give you more energy, make you smarter, and turn straw into gold. (Okay, I made up that last one, but frankly, I think it is about as likely to happen as the first two. Mostly the only thing those specialty waters do is magickally turn your money into someone else's money.)

Instead, why not create some super-duper water of your own, powered by magick and the energy of the natural world?

Take a crystal or a few special stones. I particularly like using quartz crystals, moonstone, amethyst, or citrine, but you can choose any kind you like. Make sure to wash the stones well, and then put them in a container of water (you can use a pitcher or something with a lid, depending on where you are going to be leaving it…I love nature, but I'm not all that fond of bugs in my water). If you want, add a few sprigs of herbs, like peppermint (for prosperity and health) or rosemary (for protection) or any edible flower petals. Rose petals are nice, but make sure that you get them from plants that haven't been sprayed with pesticides. Most store-bought flowers aren't good for this use, unfortunately, because you can't be sure they are safe. Sometimes you can find edible flowers in the produce aisle.

Once you have everything you want in your container, add the purest water you can find. Using your athame, a wand, or a wooden spoon, stir the contents nine times in a clockwise motion, concentrating all your intent on the positive energy of the stones and anything else you added, and having that energy move into the water. Say the following:

> All that is nature is as one. As the gods have formed the rock and the
> plant, so they have made the water. Let them be joined together for my
> positive and beneficial use.

Place the container outside in the moonlight or on a moonlit windowsill or on your altar. If none of these are available, you can set it on a countertop or table where it can stay for at least twenty-four hours. Then remove all the added items, straining the water if necessary. If you had herbs or flower petals in it, you might want to keep it in the refrigerator; otherwise, you can leave it on your altar if you like.

Whenever you need a boost, take a sip or two of the water and feel the power that comes from the natural world. It may not have the same effect as a jolt of storebought water with caffeine added to it, but it will undoubtedly be better for your spirit—and your wallet.

MAKING THE CONNECTION

Because water is everywhere, the power of the element of water is also available to you on a daily basis. It only requires mindfulness and intent on your part to take a simple cup of tea and turn it into magick, or make your evening shower a way to energetically cleanse yourself of the day's stresses. One of my favorite everyday uses for magickal water is to keep a bowl of water by the front door. Every time you come in from outside, dip your hands in the water and visualize any negativity you picked up being siphoned off harmlessly into the water. When it gets dirty (and it will), simply replace it with a new bowl. And be sure to say thank you to the power of water for helping to keep you safe and your home clear and clean.

Celebrating the Sabbats Simply

The Wheel of the Year is more than just the seasonal changes from spring to summer to fall to winter. It also encompasses the eight holidays, or sabbats: Imbolc, Ostara (the Spring Equinox), Beltane, Litha (Midsummer, or the Summer Solstice), Lammas, Mabon (the Autumnal Equinox), Samhain, and Yule (the Winter Solstice). Each of these holidays has its own energy and its own place in the cycle that influences how we practice our Craft on those days.

There are lots of books, including my own, which go into great detail about the sabbats, so I'm not going to do that here. Instead, I'm going to suggest that you take the energy of the sabbats and spread it out to cover the days and weeks that make up that season, using the ebb and flow of the Wheel of the Year to help guide your actions.

IMBOLC (FEBRUARY 2)—Many parts of the country are still deep in winter, yet this sabbat celebrates the stirring of the first life under the ground. This is still the middle of the cold and dark season, and not a time for action—not yet. Imbolc is the perfect time to make plans for the rest of the year, so you might want to make a list of your goals, both magickal and mundane, and start visualizing them or place the list on your altar and light a candle every day until the Spring Equinox.

OSTARA (AROUND MARCH 21)—The Spring Equinox is the time when life begins to return to the world—perfect for starting new endeavors and planting the seeds for your work throughout the year to come. Magick for new beginnings can be done now, and if you wrote a list of goals, you can copy it onto a piece of paper and plant some actual seeds on top of it. Be sure to water it! Don't forget to start doing practical work on your goals now, too. You don't have to accomplish everything at once, but it is time to stop dreaming and start doing.

BELTANE (MAY 1)—This sabbat celebrates the marriage of the Goddess and the God, with roots going back to early fertility rites. You don't need to run wild and have sex in the fields, but this is a time to embrace love and joy and renewal. Check in on your goals; you should be showing some progress by now. If you're not, you may want to reassess either the goals themselves or how you are going about trying to accomplish them.

LITHA (AROUND JUNE 21)—The Summer Solstice, or Midsummer, is the longest day of the year. Despite its name, it is the beginning of the summer, not the middle, but it marks the height of the year's energy. Your plans should be in full flow now, and lots of your own energy should be going into making them happen. Tap into the abundance of light and growth around you to help boost your focus and power. You can also do magick for prosperity, abundance, fertility, or love.

LAMMAS (AUGUST 1)—Lammas is the first of three Pagan harvest festivals. You should be starting to see a harvest of your efforts, too, and hopefully some of your goals have been achieved or are getting closer. If not, this is the time to reassess again and maybe change course one last time.

MABON (AROUND SEPTEMBER 21)—The Autumn Equinox is the second harvest festival and the second day in the year where the light and the darkness are in perfect balance (the Spring Equinox is the other). Now we move away from the light and into the darkness, and the falling leaves remind us that the time of abundance is coming to an end. Check back in on your goals and see how far you've come. Will you harvest the things you'd hoped for? If life doesn't seem to be going quite the way you wanted it to, now is a good time to do magick for balance, taking advantage of the sabbat's energy.

SAMHAIN (OCTOBER 31)—Samhain is the third and final harvest festival, considered by some to be the Witches' New Year. We gather in the last of the crops and tidy up the loose ends on the goals we were striving for, celebrating what we have accomplished and looking at what we didn't with an eye toward continuing that work in the new year.

YULE (AROUND DECEMBER 21)—Yule is another name for the Winter Solstice, always a time for merriment and celebration—usually with friends and family (even if they aren't Pagan). The Winter Solstice marks the longest night and the shortest day of the year. Light a fire or lots of candles (if you can safely do so) to welcome back the light and celebrate the turning of the Wheel.

I found a book recently that does a great job of helping us to tap into the flowing Wheel's energy, and it has the added benefit of being a daily devotional as well, so all the suggestions are already put into order for you. (Although, of course, you don't have to do every single thing on the day that is suggested for it.) *Living Earth Devotional: 365 Green Practices for Sacred Connection* is divided into eight sections, starting on October 31 with Samhain. The author, Clea Danaan, then lays out a season's worth of ecologically minded spirituality, tying each day's activity into the life force of that particular season. Even if you can't do each and every activity, just reading about them helps you to tune in far beyond the usual one-day celebration of each sabbat.

After all, we're trying to live our magickal practice every day, so why not take a different look at the sabbats and integrate them into our everyday practice as well?

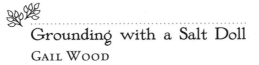

Grounding with a Salt Doll
GAIL WOOD

Staying grounded and being grounded in the heart of Mother Earth is very important in the practice of Witchcraft and one of the important things I have learned and passed on to my students. I have developed a variety of ways to ground quickly and easily. It's especially important in times of stress when doing spellwork or living our lives. Let's face it: it's important all the time!

One year, while attending a festival, I found a vendor selling little dolls that were containers of salt. The seller told me they were for grounding. The doll fits in the palm of my hand and she has long yarn hair. Holding it and stroking her hair is very comforting, and the salt purifies our pains, sorrows, and worries as she gives us a new connection to the Goddess. I have used my little salt doll in my own magic, and my circle has come to view her as a dear companion.

After some web-based research, I found that there wasn't anything written on this custom, and so we make it our own in the tradition of making meaning and in our own becoming.

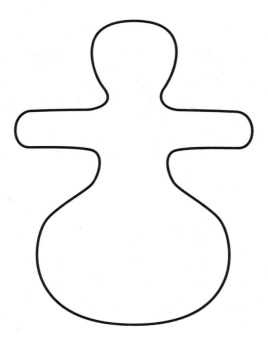

How to Make a Salt Doll

INGREDIENTS:

- 2 pieces of approximately 7 x 7-inch fabric

- 1–2 cups fine-grained salt

- yarn, floss, or other items for hair

- sewing materials: pen, machine, iron, knitting needle or other tool for turning

- doll template such as the one here

INSTRUCTIONS

1. Cut out the template on the lines.

2. Place the two smoothly ironed pieces of fabric out on a table with right sides together.

3. Trace the template on the wrong side of the fabric stack.

4. Sew along the traced lines, leaving a space open at the head.

5. Reinforce (stitch again) underneath the arms.

6. Cut out the doll, leaving approximately ¼ inch between cutting and stitching lines.

7. Turn the doll so that the right sides are on the outside—it's easier if you pull the bottommost part through first.

8. Use the top end of a knitting needle to push out the arms and smooth out the seams.

9. Fill with salt; you will need to massage the salt through the head and into the arms. Pack it as tight as you can; it takes a surprising amount.

10. Loop the yarn into a sufficient amount and insert into the top of the head.

11. Turn the edges over and sew the opening shut.

Congratulations! You are done!

You may wish to consecrate your doll. Here is a little charm to send her on her way:

> Gracious Being of Spirit and Light
> Bless this doll of fabric, yarn, and salt
> May she purify all my tears and faults
> Into the peace, joy, and delight.
> I consecrate her to the Mystery
> And to Magic and to Wonder.
> As I will it, so mote it be!

With a Little Help from My Friends

For many Pagans, the practice of Witchcraft is a solitary pursuit. Sometimes that's by choice. Sometimes it is due to a lack of anyone to practice with. The two women who started Blue Moon Circle with me had both been Solitaries for many years, in part because they were content practicing on their own and in part because they'd never found a group that was right for them.

For others, ritual is a shared experience, done in a coven or circle or even a large gathering of mostly strangers. Group work doesn't necessarily mean a crowd; I have one pal who commonly shares her ritual work with her best friend. Blue Moon Circle has varied in size over the years from three to nine, with many sabbat celebrations including a number of additional guests.

So how do you decide if you want to share your practice of the Craft with others, and how does it work if you do?

Shared Celebrations and Group Practice

Practicing the Craft with someone else can be both challenging and rewarding. The energy generated by more than one person is a very different thing than the energy you generate working on your own. It can be extremely powerful and extremely moving—as long as you are working with the right bunch of people.

Of course, it isn't always easy to find the right people. I've gone to rituals where the folks leading the rite were so scattered and unfocused, we might as well not have been in circle at all. I've been to rituals where people came to circle stoned or drunk (which not only affects the energy of the entire circle, but is, in my opinion, an insult to the gods) or chatted throughout the entire thing. Some large public rituals can be very effective…unless you happen to be stuck standing next to someone unpleasant.

On the other hand, those occasions have been the exception, not the rule. I have had amazing experiences both in my first group and at open rituals at Pagan Pride Days, Pantheacon, and large regional gatherings near my area. Some of these have been truly amazing.

The only thing better has been practicing with my own coven, Blue Moon Circle. We began working together at the 2004 Spring Equinox, and despite the many challenges that face any group, we are still together today. Some of the faces are the same and some have changed, but we are still a close-knit group of women who are more like family than we are simply a group of Witches who happen to meet on the full moons and the sabbats.

If you're lucky, you can find a group that suits you, or if you happen to know other Pagans who are also at loose ends, you might consider starting your own group. If you are all beginners, this can be tough, but there are plenty of books out there to help, including my book *Circle, Coven & Grove* and a few other books listed at the back of this one.

There are lots of things to consider, whether you are looking at joining a group or starting your own (or even if you are already in one and it is time for some changes). The most important aspects, though, are whether or not a group practice makes you happy, satisfies your spiritual needs, and helps you move forward on your path as an everyday Witch.

If you are already practicing with a coven of your own, it is probably good to occasionally check in with each other and make sure that you are all still getting these things from your work together. If the answer turns out to be no (as it will, eventually, in almost any group), a strong and healthy group will work together to find ways to revise and recharge their practice, changing those things that aren't working and celebrating those things that are.

As with any relationship, communication is absolutely vital, and both the leader (or leaders) and the participants must be willing to speak up when something isn't going well, listen to the opinions and desires of the others involved, and compromise if necessary.

Something to consider, though, is that covens (or even miscellaneous groups of witchy friends) aren't just for celebrating the sabbats and the full moons. You can get together with these folks for all sorts of more mundane activities and simply enjoy being with people who follow the same path as you do. This is not only fun, but it also builds community and creates closer bonds. (It can also give you ways to include significant others or family members who aren't comfortable with magickal work.)

For instance, I mentioned that Blue Moon Circle used to take camping trips together and go to a Renaissance Faire. There is also a local faerie festival that attracts Pagans and non-Pagans alike where you are always likely to run into someone else wearing a pentacle.

If you have a group of Pagans you enjoy spending time with, you may want to consider expanding your interactions from the spiritual to the mundane or mixing the two. Have a feast to celebrate a circle member's birthday or some notable achievement. If you have a number of members or witchy friends with small children, get together for some Pagan-centric storytelling. Have a movie night featuring your favorite films about Witches. Or just get together and have fun, knowing you are with others who accept you for exactly who you are.

Learning and Teaching: Taking Your Place in the Circle

We all start out as beginners when we walk this path. As time passes, we learn more and more about our Craft, whether that knowledge is passed down from an elder or learned from others in the community or gathered by attending classes, workshops, and rituals; studying with a high priestess or high priest; reading and researching; and just plain trial and error.

It used to be traditional for a neophyte Wiccan to study for a year and a day, receive a First Degree, study for another year and a day to achieve Second Degree status, and then, after a third year and a day, become a high priest or high priestess in their own right. After that, they often formed their own coven in a process called "hiving off." (In some traditions it might take even longer.)

These days, things are often less formal (Blue Moon Circle doesn't use a degree system of any kind, and no one but me has *any* desire to be a high priestess). Solitaries sometimes don't get the chance to study with others at all. But one thing is always true: just as we were all once new to the path, others have followed in our footsteps and now seek wisdom and guidance just as we once did.

It is just my personal opinion, but I have always felt that if we benefited at all from someone else's wisdom along the path (and even if you only learned from books, somebody sure as heck wrote them, sharing what they learned), it is part of our spiritual obligation to eventually pass some of that knowledge on to someone else.

I ended up writing my first book (*Circle, Coven & Grove: A Year of Magickal Practice*) because I had started leading Blue Moon Circle and really could have used someone to tell me what the heck I was supposed to be doing. Barring that, I looked for a book that had everything laid out for the first year of a coven's new practice: full moon, new moon, and sabbat rituals, plus some general suggestions and advice for working together. I couldn't find the book I was looking for…so, eventually, I wrote it.

I'm not necessarily suggesting that you have to write a book or even a blog post in order to share whatever knowledge you've gathered over the years. What I am suggesting is that we are essentially a small community, and there are very few places for most of us to turn when we are searching for enlightenment. And if you believe in paying it forward, as I do, passing on your own hard-earned lessons is a good way to do so.

There are various ways to take your place in the circle, and you will have to decide which ones are right for you based on a number of variables, including how open you are about your practice of the Craft, how comfortable you are teaching others, and what the need is. Maybe no one will ever ask you for help; maybe many will.

I wrote my fourth book, *The Everyday Witch A to Z Spellbook*, because I kept getting letters from people asking for practical, everyday spells they couldn't find anywhere else. ("Jerk Avoidance," anyone? Or "Potty Training"?) As a Witch with a reasonably high profile because of my books, people feel free to ask me for all sorts of advice. But if you are at all open about being a Witch, Pagan, or Wiccan, people are going to eventually ask you questions.

Here are a few ways you can take your place in the circle of knowledge:

- Answer questions if people ask you about Witchcraft—try to be tolerant of others' beliefs while explaining your own. Be as nonthreatening as possible with non-Pagans, and remember that most of what they know is based on bad movies and age-old religious propaganda.

- Explain things to new Witches if they approach you. Remember that you were once a newbie too. If you don't know the answers, try directing them to your favorite books, websites, or authors. Or just say, "I don't know the answer—let's see if we can find out."

- If you have been practicing for some time and know other local Pagans who are willing to take part, consider putting on a ritual and opening it up to either other local Witches or the public in general (depending on your comfort level and the community you live in). My former high priestess used to lead open sabbat rituals at the Unitarian Church in town, and part of my training as a high priestess was to write and present one of those. It was a truly remarkable experience that was very different from putting on a ritual for Pagans alone, and it was rewarding in an entirely different way. Lots of people who came to those open rituals said they had no idea how uplifting such a thing could be until they took part in one. Community outreach! These kinds of rituals may be the only way for some Pagans to find their own kind.

- If you are out of the broom closet, talk to people openly (in person and online) about your spiritual beliefs as a Witch. I'm not talking about inserting "I am a Witch" into every conversation, especially if it is just people talking about going to the dentist. But if it is appropriate, be open about your own particular path. The more of us who are out there talking about our beliefs on a regular basis, the more "normal" Pagan beliefs will become.

- Be a good example of what it is to be a Witch. Most other religions don't have the absurd amount of prejudice and sheer misinformation to combat that we do as Pagans. So be yourself—your BEST self—if you are presenting yourself as a Witch in front of others. Because for better or for worse, the next Witch someone meets will be walking in your shadow.

My point, really, is that if you are comfortable teaching others on any level, it is probably a good thing to do so—not necessarily in the first year of your practice, and maybe not even in the second. But once you feel you have something to share with others, I suspect you will find those who are eagerly awaiting someone to teach them. And that's the way the circle turns.

Simple Ways to Let Others In On the Wonderful World of Witchcraft (Without Scaring Them)

For most of us, the majority of the people in our lives follow some spiritual path that is different from the one we follow. That is neither a good thing nor a bad thing; it is simply the reality of being a Witch. But that doesn't mean you can't find ways to share your path some of the time, with some of the people.

For instance, when Blue Moon Circle celebrates the sabbats (as opposed to the full moons, which we keep for Witches only), we always have a ritual followed by a feast. We not only invite other Pagans to some of these occasions, but Blue Moon members are welcome to bring their families and, sometimes, interested friends.

Admittedly, we are already a family-oriented group, to the point where we have actually taken vacations together with people's kids and husbands. But beyond that, the sabbats (being as much about celebration as they are about magick, at least the way we do them) are a reasonably mellow way to share our witchy selves with the mundane folks in our lives.

One woman's husband, who has no problem with her being a Witch but is uncomfortable taking part in ritual himself, comes just for the feast. That's fine, too. The other husbands and significant others are what I'd call "Pagan friendly" (they have Pagan leanings but don't actually practice) and are happy to come stand in circle.

If the people close to you aren't comfortable coming to rituals or if you are a Solitary who has no desire to include others in your practice, there are other ways to share your witchy path with others.

Celebrate Holidays That Are Familiar

The easiest example is Yule. Blue Moon Circle has a Yule dinner party every year—an actual sit-down, fancy-pants kind of dinner where people dress up and we all sit around the table instead of in the living room with paper plates perched on our knees. We invite friends to this who might not otherwise come to rituals, in part because Christmas traditions are so close to Yule's (since most of them were appropriated from the Pagans in the first place), and therefore they are more likely to be comfortable.

You can have a Yule party or a Winter Solstice gathering (I even know non-Pagans who have Solstice parties) and invite anyone you think might be open to seeing the similarities between the two holidays. Have a Yule tree instead of a Christmas tree, and decorate it with Pagan or witchy symbols. If you want to have a hands-on kind of gathering, get some fun supplies together and have people make their own ornaments to hang on the tree: stars with their wishes written on them, for instance, or edible garlands made of popcorn and cranberries.

If you will be gathering around a dinner table, you can make cards to put at each person's place with interesting or amusing facts about the holiday, and your guests can take turns reading them out loud. Consider including the following items (or anything else that strikes your fancy):

- The green and red colors traditionally associated with Christmas come from the colors of the holly.

- Evergreen trees and swags were brought into the house to symbolize life in the midst of death during the cold, dark season.

- The Solstice celebrates the return of the light (the sun), since it is the turning point in the year where the days become a little longer as the months progress toward spring.

- Most countries have some form of "Santa Claus": a bearded old man who comes bringing presents. It is thought that this may stem from the Pagan Oak King and Holly King, each of whom rules over half of the year. The Holly King, who rules over the dark half of the year, is overthrown at Yule by his brother, the Oak King.

- Yule was originally a very raucous and rowdy holiday. People would "go a-wassailing" from neighbor's house to neighbor's house, singing songs and drinking at each place. The celebration was so wild, the church tried to ban it. In the end, they mostly adopted some of the less boisterous aspects of the holiday, and it became the one we are familiar with today.

- If you listen to many traditional carols, they include words or terms that are clues to the Pagan origins of the holiday, such as "Yuletide merry" and "we will go a-wassailing." (You can see how many carols people can come up with that fit this description, and the person who thinks of the most can win a prize.)

You get the idea. If you do a little research, you can come up with plenty of fun facts about the holiday to share with those who know little about the origins of the Christian holiday so many people celebrate today.

Other fun activities to do at a Yule party might include making edible decorations to hang outside for the birds (try covering pine cones or apples with peanut butter and then rolling them in birdseed; they can then be hung from trees or bushes), singing Pagan versions of Christmas carols (check YouTube for ideas), and having a couple of children act out the battle between the Oak King and the Holly King, with the victor giving out small gifts to all the guests once he is crowned.

Any of the Solstices (Winter or Summer) or Equinoxes (Fall or Spring) are good occasions to share with non-witchy friends or family, since most people are familiar with the concept.

The Spring Equinox, in particular, otherwise known as Ostara, is a good choice because of its many similarities to the Christian Easter. (Obviously, this was another holiday where they borrowed heavily from Pagan traditions, including using fertility symbols like chicks and bunnies and eggs.) Both holidays celebrate birth, rebirth, and hope.

Imbolc, which has been adapted in modern times to the more familiar Groundhog's Day, is another holiday where you could point out a similar theme: the anticipation of the coming of spring.

You don't necessarily have to do anything formal, either. Host a May Day or Summer Solstice barbecue or a harvest festival potluck focused on foods grown locally.

Use your imagination and have fun. Invite people who you know are interested and open-minded, and keep in mind that the occasion is all about sharing information and having a good time, not pushing your views or religion on others or putting down anyone else's beliefs or religion.

Give a Non-Threatening Explanation of Craft Basics

One of the ways in which Witchcraft differs from other religions is that we don't proselytize (try to persuade other people to join our religion). In fact, in the early days of Wicca, there was one tradition that said a person had to ask three times to come to a coven before they were even allowed to attend a ritual. We tend to be a little more relaxed these days and often invite people we think might have Pagan leanings, but we're not, in general, a religious group that tries to recruit people to "convert" to our way of doing things.

In fact, one of the aspects of Paganism that appeals to me the most is that—again, generally speaking—Witches tend not to take the "we're the only right way" attitude, instead simply wishing to be left alone to practice as we wish.

But this same hands-off approach has one disadvantage, which is that most people only get their knowledge of modern Witchcraft from bad television and worse movies or age-old anti-Witch propaganda that was part of the political power plays of days long gone by. So if you get the chance to *gently* share some more accurate information, this can only be a good thing for all of us.

There are a few things you might want to keep in mind while you are giving people a glimpse of the wonderful world of Witchcraft.

- Not everyone is interested. Some folks don't like to talk about religion or spirituality at all, and others are too prejudiced to change their views, no matter what you say, or they are simply uncomfortable with alternative religions. Save your energy to talk to someone else.

- If people express interest or give you some kind of an opening for discussion, go slowly, and don't dump a lot of information on them at once. For instance, people often notice when I am wearing a pentacle and may say, "Hey, isn't that one of those Witch symbols?" In which case I explain to them about the five points representing the five elements of earth, air, fire, water, and spirit, and the circle of unity/the universe that ties them all together. For some folks, that is all the information they want, so I let it go at that. Others are clearly intrigued, so, depending on the situation, I may move on to discuss Witchcraft in more depth. (Note the word "discuss"—you want to have a conversation with give and take, not just a lecture from you.)

- If someone asks me if I am a Witch, I always say, "Yes, in fact, I am." Sometimes I make a joke to put them at ease, such as, "But don't worry, I'm a good Witch, not a bad Witch" or "It's okay—I haven't turned anyone into a toad in years." Many people still find Witches a little scary, so it never hurts to inject some humor into the conversation.

- If you don't know where to start when someone asks you about the practice of Witchcraft, you can always begin by saying it is a nature-based religion. This often puts people at ease. I go on to explain that it is based, at least loosely, on Pagan practices that many of our ancestors followed at one point or another, and that we follow natural cycles and try to stay in tune with the natural energies of the seasons, and so on.

- You can also explain that most Witches believe in both a God and a Goddess as a reflection of the male and female that can be found elsewhere in the natural world. It is sometimes helpful to point out that Christianity has Mary, who—while not viewed as a goddess— is a very powerful and important part of their worship, or mention Brigid, who is both a goddess and a saint. I often express my belief that all deity springs from the same source, and that each of us finds a way to connect with it/him/her that suits us best.

- People often ask me if Witches really do magick. This is an area that a lot of people are curious about and/or have serious misconceptions concerning. It can also be a little tricky to explain magick to people who have never used it. I usually try to keep it simple: I say that Witches believe that magick is just another force in the universe (like any other source of energy) that we can tap into to help us create positive change. You can point out that prayer and spells have a lot in common—they are both ways of asking for help—or that other religions use ritual in one form or another (Catholic mass is a ritual, for instance, as are many Jewish practices). Pagans just have a different approach.

Keep in mind that you are trying to spread information and under-standing, not start an argument about whose religion is better. If someone responds by becoming antagonistic or appears uncomfortable, you can sim-ply agree to disagree and change the subject.

Sharing Witchcraft with the Younger Set

If you or people in your coven have children, you may want to involve them in some witchy activities. You can include them in ritual or find other less formal ways to introduce them to their first taste of the Pagan experience.

(Just a note: NEVER involve someone else's children without the par-ents' permission. If you have a significant other who is firmly against Witchcraft, you may want to wait or at least proceed with caution, espe-cially if there is a divorce involved. It is sad but true that in this day and age, people can still have their children taken away from them by a judge if an opposing parent can convince the court that the children are being exposed to something dangerous. Use caution if you are in a tricky situa-tion. Ditto if someone else's teen comes to you and wants to learn without a parent's permission. You have to use your own best judgment in cases like these.)

Nature is a perfect venue for beginning an exploration of Pagan thoughts and practices. Depending on the age of the child, you can come up with various crafts and activities that provide ways to interact with and connect to nature, and perhaps explain as you do them a little something about the history of Pagans and their connection to the land.

Make birdfeeders or birdhouses, start a small garden, go for a walk in the woods—it doesn't have to be complicated or expensive. Integrate music such as chanting, drumming, or playing a simple flute. Rattles are a great musical instrument for small children, and there are some easy ones you can make yourself. (Dried beans in an empty container with a lid—*poof*, instant rattle!)

Try discussing the elements and doing projects that address each one. What child doesn't like to play with water? You don't necessarily need to invent new activities; just figure out how to take things you already do and give them a witchy slant. Flying a kite, for instance, can be a way to commune with air, and picking up pretty rocks or a special branch to make into a wand can lead to a discussion of earth. Need a good activity for fire? Try roasting marshmallows carefully over an open flame.

If you have children (or even if you don't), you may want to integrate a witchy element into fun and relaxing activities. Put out food for the faeries while you tend the garden. Send wishes out into the universe as you blow bubbles or draw magickal symbols on the ground with colored chalk. And don't forget to tell wonderful magickal stories through song and chanting.

Obviously, the age and interest level of the children involved (and how deeply you want to delve into the world of Witchcraft with them) will determine, to some extent, what kind of activities you want to do. But in general, the sky's the limit.

Don't forget to take advantage of books while you are at it. There are plenty of great stories about some of the gods, especially Greek, Roman, Celtic, and Egyptian ones, as well as many fairy tales that have a Pagan flair. There are also some fictional books about Witches that don't feature Witches as scary old women who eat children, although most of them don't talk about modern Witches in any kind of realistic manner, of course. (Last time I checked, my kind of magick bore very little resemblance to that wielded by Harry Potter, alas.)

There are also some great books for people who want ideas for sharing their spiritual practice with their children. I've listed a few at the back of the book.

It's All About Connection

Regardless of whether you are working with a group of like-minded Witches, sharing your knowledge with those seeking to learn more, or sharing your spiritual practice with friends and family, it all comes down to connection.

To me, that is what being a Witch is all about: connecting with nature, yes; connecting with the God and Goddess, definitely; and also connecting with other people in a positive and uplifting way—coming together to celebrate, to learn, and to create. Even a Solitary Witch interacts with others from time to time, even if not during her practice of Witchcraft.

I encourage you to find new and wonderful ways to make this connection on one level or another. You might be surprised by how much joy you will find.

Including Special-Needs Children in Ritual
Kris Bradley

My middle child was diagnosed on the autism spectrum at three years old. As my son grew, we struggled to find a place where both he and I were comfortable socializing. Things have improved a lot over the last decade as far as awareness and inclusion, but there is still work to be done.

As parents of kids with special needs, we so often have to see our kids passed over. There are a million little disappointments for our kids, and any person or group that gives them the chance to participate and shine is going to have our love and loyalty. Whether you are an individual trying to include a friend's child with autism into your sabbat celebration or you are working to plan a large event such as a Pagan Pride function, here are a few ideas to get you started on creating an inclusive gathering.

Obviously, every special-needs child (and adult) will have different needs. Communication between the event planner and the hopeful attendees is so very important; it also needs to go in both directions. As parents, we need to step up and let our friends and our event coordinators know that our kids are coming and start a conversation on what it would take for our kids to be able to participate. At the same time, we also have to realize that compromise is going to be key. Even better, volunteer for the planning stages so that making changes toward inclusion becomes a priority.

There are many people who have kids with differences who just give up on the idea of being able to attend events. If you are planning something small, just ask your friends how best to include their children and really listen to what they are telling you.

If you are helping to organize a larger event, start at the very beginning by adding a contact person as a special-needs coordinator (for all ages). Consider having a "quiet area" for kids who are overwhelmed by all the noise and bustle, and remember the "three S" plan: keep it short, simple, and similar.

Though every group of kids is going to be different, keeping things short will help keep their attention focused. Keep it simple: keep the language simple to understand and simplify the steps as much as possible. I have a friend who is on the autism spectrum who helps her parents call the quarters during ritual with a simple call of "Hi, air!"

That brings us to keeping it similar. All kids like to know what they are in store for, but for many kids with special needs, it's the difference between having a successful outing or not. Repeat ritual elements from year to year and, if possible, send out an email notice 2–3 weeks before the event, with a short rundown of the event so that parents can start prepping the kids who need it.

If you can, give each child a "job" during ritual. Offer every child in attendance a way to participate, whether you cast the circle "conga-line" style (letting everyone move around the circle) or in a small group (allowing everyone a speaking part in calling quarters). If there are nonverbal participants, give them a drum to beat or a rattle to shake or have them call using sign language. If you aren't sure what job works best for each child, ask the parents ahead of time.

Lastly, please consider your location when making plans, and make it as accessible as possible. As more and more families every year are working around the special needs of their children, and as more families are finding their faith under the Pagan umbrella, it's so important for us to bring those two worlds together and celebrate Pagans of every ability.

CHAPTER 6

Good Ritual

Z BUDAPEST

It has been many years since I began teaching about women making ritual together. Every book I have written since (nine titles) contains some more information: how to adjust the rituals to different purposes; how to bend it, vary it, and still have it down solid. I have ordained twelve high priestesses who, in turn, have ordained others. The sacred work of women's mysteries is happening nicely all over the world.

Every so often I go to a circle and have a reality check. Many women's circles are satisfied with just the "clinical" variety—a workshop parading as a circle. Good intentions are not enough here. You either deliver a spiritual power-raising experience or you teach about it only. One is called a sacred circle; the other is called a workshop. Yes, the two can follow each other, but they cannot occur at the same time.

There is a huge difference between a workshop and a ritual. But we need them both. Let me explain.

In a workshop the left brain is engaged. The workshop teaches skills. There is a lot of talk: there may be a book reading involved or sharing stories, talking, writing on little pieces of paper, burning them, sending around a mirror or a bowl of water, changing the activity into something else. Focusing the attention of the women on an aspect of the Goddess and getting deeper—all this is workshopping.

We need this in the beginning stages of the Path. We need to refurbish our minds with the ancient mythology; we need to learn the aspects of the Goddess, she of the ten thousand names. A workshop is like going to a good magic school.

Then what is the circle? It's a temple that is portable. It is a fresh encounter with the divine feminine. It's a structured event where we have to dress up the form with all contributing. There is a leader of energies, the high priestess. Like the conductor of an orchestra, a good high priestess employs us in the circle according to our strengths and asks us to contribute without disrupting the right-brain activities.

118

A good ritual uses mostly the right brain—the old brain. This is where all our genetic memories are kept. This is where words have little meaning, only chanting, singing, scents, dances, touching, eating, dancing, kissing. A good ritual shouldn't last longer than an hour. Anything that goes beyond an hour will crash the energies.

Every step has to give way to the next step; it has to hang together like a well-made macramé. Just like the dark space that holds the visible universe together, the high priestess's watchful instincts hold together the energy of the circle.

A good ritual has a definite beginning, a middle with a purpose, and a satisfying, well-grounded end. I bring magical play to the circle, which engages the women. I call out, "The goddess is alive!" and they answer, "Magic is afoot." Then we each say our names—"Z is alive"—and after each name everybody answers, "Magic is afoot!" It takes a little time to say all of our names if the circle is large, but it is still active, and everyone is engaged.

Then there is the candle-lighting-with-wishes part, which is normally the middle of a circle. Women come to ask for help in their lives, which is the role of good spirituality: give a framework for humans to ask for divine intervention. This is known as the power of prayer in all religions. In ours we do it while lighting an appropriately colored candle, and we open our arms and pray from the heart.

The end of the ritual also must be organic. You will feel when the energy is waning; you don't wait until it all runs out of steam. You create a power cone again, pulling together; at the end, the energy should peak. So let it soar! The closing part of the circle is love. You either hug each other in a group hug, which is very grounding, or you proceed to have the feast for the Goddess, which also will beautifully ground you.

So please be clear on whether you are having a circle or a workshop.

We must develop and insist on higher-quality food for our souls. It takes a little devotion, a little good will, and a divine sense of the fleeting sacred. This is a good ritual.

Fur, Feather, and Fang

While it isn't true for everyone, many Pagans and Witches have a strong connection with animals. Most of the witchy folks I know tend to have a bunch of critters—cats, dogs, birds, lizards, snakes…you name it, I know a Pagan who's got one (or more than one).

I'm not sure exactly why this is. Maybe it has something to do with our being a nature-based religion, because animals are a very relatable part of nature. Maybe we're all just big softies. Mostly, I think it is because we are so open to connection in general: connection with deity, the natural world, spirit…and animals are a part of all that. And, of course, it is traditional for a Witch to have a familiar, although not all of them do.

Different Witches relate to animals in different ways. Some simply have pets (or, as they are known in my house, Feline Overlords) who provide comfort and companionship. Others have actual familiars who are involved with their magickal workings. Many Pagans have power animals or animal totems who lend them strength and guidance, and there are even a small number of Pagans who identify as Theriantropes or Otherkin, which, as I understand it, means that they feel they are animal beings in human-shaped bodies.

No matter how you choose to approach your interactions with those of fur, feather, and fang, they can add another dimension to both your life and your magickal practice.

Pets and Familiars

Pets are a great conduit into the natural world. Whether you prefer the traditional Witch's black cat or a wriggly puppy or something more exotic, like a snake (or something less exotic, like a hamster), pets give us a way to make a connection to something more basic and honest than the lives that humans lead.

Having a pet is a commitment, though, and not something to be undertaken lightly. Unlike some other religions that see the natural world, and therefore all animals, as things that *belong* to humankind (that is to say, something we own, to do with as we will), Pagans take a different view. We tend to see the natural world as a gift we are allowed to enjoy, but not something that belongs to us.

The same applies to animals. They are not possessions to be acquired and tossed away like pieces of furniture. Instead, most Witches believe that animals are also children of the God and Goddess. If we are fortunate enough to share our homes with one or more of them, we owe them the best care possible, and we treat them with kindness and respect. They are our furry brothers and sisters, not our slaves.

I have five cats, but only one of them is a true familiar. There is one thing you need to know about familiars: you don't choose them, *they* choose *you*. (There are some folks who feel that this is true of companion animals in general, especially cats and dogs.)

What I mean by this is that you can't set out to find a familiar. You can ask the gods to send you one if you feel the need for an animal to share your magickal practice, but there is no point in going out and getting a pet specifically so you can have a familiar. Yes, if you feel drawn to an animal, by all means adopt him or her if you have the resources to take care of the critter in question, but don't be disappointed if you get your cat/dog/lizard/gerbil home and he is completely uninterested in taking part in your spiritual activities. Never get an animal if you will not want it for itself alone.

Those of you who are familiar with my work, whether it is my previous books or my ongoing blog, will know that Magic the Cat, Queen of the Universe, is a familiar in the truest sense of the word. If I am doing magickal work, she almost always shows up.

I don't do anything to make her be in the room with me. She's a cat; she goes wherever she wants. But when Blue Moon Circle and I gather in the living room because the weather prevents us from being outside, Magic always makes an appearance. *Always.* We start off chatting, but sooner or later we stand, light the sage, and cast the circle. We know that we are in sacred space when Magic shows up.

She strolls into the room as if she owns it, walks around the circle (deosil, or clockwise, of course), greets everyone, and then either settles onto the floor under the altar table or perches on the couch to supervise. When we're done, she leaves the room.

When I do magickal work on my own, she usually shows up around the time I start saying a spell and often yowls along with me. Does her presence make my work stronger? I have to assume it does. Either way, she clearly senses something out of the ordinary—something that the other cats either don't feel or choose to ignore.

Interestingly, she also helps out when I am doing energy-healing work (often sitting on the person I am working on, and almost always finding the spot that needs the most help), and she sometimes comes to sit on the dining room table when I am giving a tarot reading. Clearly, she is in tune with all kinds of unusual energy. A couple of the other cats occasionally show interest in either the magickal work or the energy work, but only Magic is consistently *there.*

Why her? How does this work?

Honestly—I don't know. I just accept it as the gift it is, with gratitude and appreciation.

I *do* know that Witches have been working with familiars for centuries. I also know that Magic found me, not the other way around.

If you want a familiar or have been getting those not-so-subtle hints from the universe that it might be time, my suggestion is that you keep your eyes and your heart open. One will probably show up when you least expect it.

A few daily activities you can do with a familiar:

- Go for a walk with your dog and try to see what he finds interesting. Maybe there is a faery hiding under a bush or some bit of nature you should be noticing.

- Watch for a cat that is looking at nothing. Sometimes Magic stares at a corner when there doesn't seem to be anything there. Can you sense some kind of energy?

- Want some help answering a question? Try putting a few tarot cards or some 3 x 5 cards with options like "yes," "no," or "wait to decide" on the floor where your familiar can reach them. Ask the question, and see if your familiar is willing to help you with an answer.

- Not feeling well? Ask your familiar to sit with you and lend you a little healing energy.

Power Animals

Many Pagans have something they call a power animal or an animal totem—an animal that has come to them during some kind of spiritual journey and attached itself in spirit form as a guide, helper, or symbol of some aspect of the user's personality, gifts, or path.

NOTE: Keep in mind that this is not particularly a Wiccan idea; in fact, if you use the word "totem," some might consider you guilty of what they call cultural appropriation (meaning you are swiping the culture that belongs to others, in this case Native Americans). Frankly, much of what we use in modern Witchcraft comes from a mishmash of various cultures, so it can be pretty hard to avoid doing that on one level or another. But if you are worried about it, you might want to stick with the terms *power animal* or *animal spirit*.

Power animals can bring very different things to different people, and their use isn't limited to Witches; many Pagans of one sort or another, including Native Americans and many other shamanic people, have a long history of connecting with animal spirits for help, guidance, and strength.

There are some animals that are traditionally associated with the role of totem or power animal. There are strength animals such as the bear, the wolf, and the eagle, or wise animals such as the owl, the coyote, and the fox. (Although many animals have more than one meaning or purpose.) And, of course, there are the mythical beasts: the phoenix (which usually symbolizes rebirth and triumph over adversity), the dragon, and the gryphon.

People tend to be attracted to the animal totem or power animal they need, but sometimes it is easy to be distracted by the ones we *think* we want/ need/should have and miss out on the ones that are really right for us.

I have a confession to make. For many years, my power animal was— wait for it—a flock of sheep. Seriously. I'd be hanging out with a bunch of other Pagans, and people would start talking about their power animals. Just visualize the following conversation:

Pagan One: *Oh, yes, my power animal is a wolf.*

Pagan Two: *Excellent! My power animal is an eagle.*
    I see them everywhere.

Pagan One: *Hey, Deborah, do you have a power animal?*

Me (*looking at the floor and mumbling*): Um, yeah. It's a flock of sheep.

[*Insert general laughter here.*]

And honestly, it *is* funny. I laugh about it myself. On the other hand, for reasons way too complicated to get into here, those were the totems I needed at that time. They stayed with me on a long, tough road and brought me a lot of comfort. I still collect little stuffed sheep if I see one that appeals to me, even though the flock has moved on and been replaced by other, more conventional guides.

My point here, besides the fact that I'm not nearly as cool as you all thought, is that you need to keep an open mind when it comes to animal totems and power animals. Just because you'd *like* something to be your power animal doesn't mean it *is*.

One way to tell is to go on a shamanic journey or ask during a hypnotherapy session (that's how I found out, in fact) or some other time when you are in an altered state of consciousness.

You can also just keep your eyes open. Many times, a power animal will show up repeatedly to tell you it belongs to you. If you keep seeing turtles everywhere you go—on the side of the road, on someone's shirt, in a magazine article—that may be the universe trying to tell you something. It is also not uncommon to dream about your animal totem. If one particular animal shows up repeatedly in your dreams, this may be a sign that it is your power animal.

If you think you have found a power animal or totem but you aren't sure, you can always do some magickal work to find out. This doesn't have to be anything complicated. You can either go outside and sit in a quiet place or cast a circle inside and light a candle, then just close your eyes and ask. If you get a clear vision of the animal, you'll know it is the one for you. If you don't, then you might not be looking at the right animal, or perhaps it just isn't in the mood to talk to you yet.

You can also ask the universe to send you a power animal or totem. Try lighting a candle and saying:

> Power animal, I call on thee
> To help me as I walk my path
> To bring me strength and clarity
> Come to me as I doth ask!

Then close your eyes and see if an image comes to you.

As with most other things in Witchcraft, you need to keep an open mind, have faith, and be patient—if there is a power animal out there for you, sooner or later, it will show up.

Just hope that when it does, it doesn't say *baaaaaaaaaaaa*.

Connecting with Animal Spirit

There are many different ways to connect with animal spirit, and not all of them will be right for you. The important thing is that you find some path toward establishing a connection that suits your own particular needs and inclinations. Here are a few suggestions to get you started:

GET A PET—If you can, adopt one that *really* needs a home. You don't need to buy a pet, but keep in mind that having one will cost money, take time and effort, and sometimes be annoying—*Magic! Get off the table right now!* Don't get a pet if you're not prepared to take on the responsibility. On the other hand, having an animal companion can be incredibly rewarding whether or not it turns out to have magickal leanings. If you like a particular kind of purebred animal, see if there is a rescue organization for that breed, which seeks homes for abandoned or abused animals.

FEED THE BIRDS OR THE CRITTERS—Whether you put up a bird feeder outside your own window or go to a nearby park to scatter nuts for the squirrels, you can derive a lot of satisfaction from helping out Mother Nature, especially during the winter, when in some places it can be hard for her creatures to find food. Just be careful that you aren't breaking any local ordinances or attracting pests. I consider feeding the birds to be part of my spiritual practice, and I am rewarded by their song and their beauty in the depths of the cold and gray months. If you own your own home, you can plant bushes and trees that bear bird-attracting fruit. (I also have deer who love the apples that fall off my apple trees. And the other day I saw a very smug crow fly off with a huge apple in its beak.)

LOOK OUT THE WINDOW—I love watching the birds out my window first thing in the morning. Where I live, out in the country, I can also see deer, woodchucks, chipmunks, rabbits, and various other wild critters. Even if you live in the city, you can probably spot some wildlife (yes, pigeons count).

GO TO THE ZOO OR AN ANIMAL PARK—If you have small kids, you can go to a petting zoo or maybe even visit a local farm.

TRY VOLUNTEERING AT A LOCAL SHELTER—If you can't have a pet but you like cats and dogs, this kind of thing is definitely work of the spirit and a gift to the Mother, as well as a good way to spend time connecting with animals.

FLY HIGHER—Do some shamanic journeying to connect with animals in the spirit realm.

As with all other facets of your spiritual and magickal work, you will undoubtedly be drawn to the path that is right for you. Use your imagination, ask the gods for guidance, and follow your heart. Animals are as much the God and Goddess's children as we are, which in some way makes them our brothers and sisters.

A (Very Brief) Introduction to Animal Totemism
LUPA

No human is an island, and neither is the entirety of humanity. We share our world with a variety of other animal species, from mynah birds to golden jackals to sarcastic fringeheads. They've fascinated us for millennia, being intimately connected to our art as cultural and spiritual symbols.

There are numerous ways to connect with animals in spirituality; one of my favorites is animal totemism. An animal totem is an archetypal being that embodies all of the qualities of a given species of animal, from natural history to mythology to the relationships that species has to other animals, humans included. So the Gray Wolf totem is made up of all the traits and behavior of all gray wolves plus all the stories and art we've created about those animals and the connections wolves have to other animals, prey and otherwise. This is a much deeper well of knowledge and experience to draw from than working with a single wolf spirit. Additionally, unlike physical animals, totems are able to communicate with us in ways that our mind and intuition can easily understand.

There's no set number of totems a person may work with; some only have one over a lifetime, while others explore spirituality with many. You may already know one or more of "your" totems; if not, here's a brief guided meditation to help you make that first connection.

Go to a quiet place where you can comfortably meditate. Take a few deep breaths and relax. Now, imagine that you're standing in front of a tunnel in the ground. Walk into that tunnel and travel through it until you emerge from the other end into a natural area—it can be any sort of natural area, from a garden to the seaside to a desert. As you explore this area, you may meet one or more animal totems; they may come and speak with you. Make note of what they say and do, and remember that this is just an introduction; you can always come back here to talk with them more and find others to work with. Once you're done talking with the totems, head back to the tunnel and return to your body. You may wish to write down or otherwise record what happened in the meditation as soon as you're "awake" again.

If you didn't meet any totems or if the meditation seemed unclear, wait a few weeks, then try again. Once you have met at least one totem, the best way to learn more about them and why they showed up in your meditation is to go back through the tunnel and speak with them more. There are several dictionaries of animal totem meanings out there, but keep in mind that those meanings are what the totems told that author; what they teach *you* may be very different.

A good thank-you gift to the totems you work with is donating time or money to nonprofit groups that benefit their physical counterparts.

Your Magickal Home

You have probably heard the expression "home is where the heart is." If you are a Witch, home is also where the spirit is.

For many Witches, their home is literally their temple: the place where they conduct most of their religious and spiritual work. Even those who go elsewhere for their large rituals almost always have at least one altar at home and do some magickal work there. If you are an everyday Witch, then many of your day-to-day activities around the house also include a hint of magick.

So how do you make your home into a temple? And once you have, how do you keep it a safe, comfortable, and powerful place to do magickal work? More than that, how do you use everyday tasks around the house to help you walk your talk every day?

I'm so glad you asked.

Sacred Space Everywhere: Making Your Home into a Magickal Place

My entire house is sacred space. In part, that is because it has great energy, some of which is generated by me, presumably, or simply is the nature of the house itself, and some of which is the result of over twelve years of constant magickal workings. If you figure a minimum of twelve full moons and eight sabbats a year plus the occasional new moon get-together, that's a *lot* of rituals, and those are only the ones I do with Blue Moon Circle. I do plenty of magickal work on my own, too. So really, my house *is* a temple.

But there's more to it than that. Some of it has to do with attitude: to me, my house is sacred space. It is my refuge from an uncertain world filled with unpleasant people and negative energy. (Not that those are the only things out there, by any means, but it is nice to have a place where you can purposefully block them out.) It is the center of my universe. And, of course, it is where my Feline Overlords rule, which makes it extra special. When I look around my house, I don't just see rooms; I see a home.

So the first place to start, if you want the place you live in to be a magickal zone, is your own attitude. Not everyone lives where they want to, unfortunately, and plenty of folks are stuck in substandard housing or in areas they'd rather not be. Nonetheless, if you are living someplace you aren't thrilled with but you're going to be stuck there for a while, you will probably want to make that space as sacred as possible. That may require a change of attitude.

I spent eleven years living in a small two-bedroom apartment with nasty old carpets and drunken landlords who lived downstairs and fought with each other all the time. It was in town (a small town, and nice, but one with two colleges and a *lot* of bars) instead of out in the country, where I prefer to live. Some nights it got very loud.

And yet, once I became a Witch, that crappy apartment was sacred space too. I did some magickal work there (although not as much, since I was just starting out), but mostly I just appreciated it for what it was: a safe place, a roof over my head, better than a lot of the alternatives, and the place I called home. The energy wasn't nearly as nice, but for the time I was there, I made the best of it.

So that's the first step to making your home sacred space: say that it is and see it through your eyes as the temple of your spiritual self. As Witches, we know that we have the power to change our reality. You can't necessarily get rid of a nasty carpet, but you can change how you *look* at that carpet, and that's a start.

The next step is to physically and psychically cleanse the place as much as you can and begin using it for magickal work. The more work you do, the more magickal energy seeps into the floorboards and the walls and the very air of your home, creating sacred space through your own use of the elements of earth, air, fire, water, and especially spirit.

And, of course, you can put up an altar or two.

Altars Inside and Out

As individual as fingerprints, altars are the visual representation of our spiritual DNA.

The dictionary I use defines an altar as a table that serves as a center for worship or ritual, but in reality, an altar can be anything from a rock set into the ground, a fancy inlaid stand, or a tiny spot atop a dresser. It can be permanent or portable, simple or ornate; every Witch's altar is different, and there is no right way to set one up or use one.

Some people mostly use their altars as a place to practice their magickal work. Others treat them as a focus for the worship of a particular god or goddess. In fact, in many cultures across the world—from Japan to Africa to Greece—altars are set up somewhere in the home to honor ancestors and the particular household gods worshiped there. Christians sometimes have home altars to Mary or a patron saint where candles are burned and prayers recited, and, of course, there are also altars in churches.

I have a number of altars, and each one has a purpose. One is a large stone slab set on the ground in the middle of the permanent magickal circle that lies out behind my barn, which Blue Moon Circle uses when we do magickal work outside. (That's our first choice, but the upstate New York weather doesn't always cooperate.) When we perform ritual in the outdoor circle, the altar is where we put items like the God and Goddess candles, a small cauldron that holds a sage smudge stick, containers of salt and water, the cakes and ale, and so on. The rest of the time it is simply a rock sitting in a circle of smaller rocks, absorbing the energy of the sun and the rain and whatever else happens to come by.

All the other altars are inside the house. One is a wooden shelf high up on the wall of the bedroom and is mostly decorative. The other working altars are in the main part of the house, where they are easy to use.

Your altar may not bear any resemblance to mine. Presumably, whether you have one or many, they will be created to suit your own needs. If you want something traditional, there are plenty of books that will tell you in great detail the "correct" placement of your magickal items. (Does the Goddess go on the left or the right? I can never remember.)

Or you can just arrange things whichever way seems most satisfying to you. Here are a few different styles and types of altar to get you started:

NONE—Okay, this may not be a type of altar, but the point here is that there is no rule that says you *have* to have one. If you're a "stand in the woods and talk to the Goddess" kind of Witch, you may decide to forgo one altogether, and that's just fine.

SIMPLE—An altar doesn't have to be fancy and complicated. If your life is rushed and hectic, and you feel overwhelmed by the necessity of taking care of one more thing, you may choose to have a simplistic altar. This can be as basic as a single candle in a spot where you will see it often and be reminded to make a connection with your witchy self. Or it may a statue or statues to your patron god/dess plus a simple symbol of each of the four elements.

INCOGNITO—Witches who are still living with the necessity of hiding their spiritual beliefs often feel that they can't have an altar, for fear that it will give them away. Luckily, since much of Witchcraft centers around nature, it is pretty easy to have an altar in disguise—one that no one but you will realize is anything other than just decoration. Try using very basic symbols for the Goddess and the God, such as a cup, bowl, or goblet for the Goddess (to represent the womb) and a stick, antler, or decorative letter opener (instead of an athame) to represent the God. For the four elements, you can use a shell or piece of sea glass for water; a stick of incense, a feather, or a wind chime for air; a candle, a red piece of stone or glass, or a hunk of volcanic rock for fire; and a rock, crystal, or plant for earth. You can easily create a small table or shelf with a few items that no one but you ever need know is magickal.

PORTABLE—Some Witches have to keep their altar supplies tucked away, either out of secrecy or to keep them away from grabby little fingers. Others like to have a small kit they can take outside whenever they do ritual. It is easy to assemble a portable altar. Start with a nice box or bag and add a lightweight cloth you can unfold and place on the ground or wherever you will be assembling your altar. My portable altar contains mini candles with mini holders, one each for the Goddess (silver), God (gold), and the four quarters (red, blue, yellow, green), as well as a small sage smudge stick, a tiny vial of premixed water and salt, a piece of chalk for drawing symbols as necessary, a small crystal, and some matches. It all fits into a velveteen bag not much larger than my palm and can easily be tucked away in a suitcase when I am traveling. You could also use many elements of the incognito altar if you want to take it with you and not have people realize what it is.

GOD/GODDESS/SPIRIT ANIMAL—You can easily create a special altar dedicated to one particular god, goddess, or power animal. Some people look for a statue that represents the deity/animal, while others use symbols customarily associated with the one the altar is for. For instance, an altar dedicated to Hecate might have a black candle, a small statue of a hound, some symbol to represent a crossroads, and a skull, whereas an altar for Demeter might have a basket filled with fruits and vegetables or a dried gourd. Do some research and find out what is most appropriate for your particular choice, and then use the bits and pieces that appeal to you most. Or ask your deity/animal what they want, and then give it to them.

THEME—As with my writing inspiration altar, you can always have an altar with a special theme. Some people like to have an altar to each element placed in the direction associated with that element.

This can change from tradition to tradition, but in mine that would mean I'd have an altar to earth on the north wall, an altar to air on the east wall, and so on. You can have any theme you want. Animal lovers might have a cat altar (my cats seem to think the entire house is an altar to them, and they're not far off); people with children might want to have a family altar, where everyone can contribute something to its creation. You might have an altar you change four times a year with the seasons or eight times a year with the sabbats. Or you can have an altar to address a particular need, desire, or something you are grateful for: love, healing, protection, etc. You can also have an altar that honors your ancestors or your beloved dead. (People often put up a temporary ancestor altar around Samhain.)

decorative—I have talked about the fact that one of my altars is simply decorative. There is nothing wrong with having an altar that exists for no other reason than to be a symbol of your faith and to add beauty to your home while also showing off your witchy self. This is a good place to put things that are lovely but not truly functional (like that carved wooden chalice you can't actually drink from) or things that need to be kept up high and safe.

WORKING—If you only have one altar, you will probably want to have one of these. This altar is the one you will use for magickal work, for prayer and contemplation, for ritual of any kind. It might be a combination of some of the others mentioned above, but it should also be functional and be placed where you will see it and be reminded on a daily basis that Witchcraft is an important part of your life. (Unless, of course, you need to hide it away, in which case it should at least be easy to grab when you suddenly have the house to yourself.) What you put on it will depend entirely on the kind of magick you practice, but it should hold at least the basics for spellwork and worship.

No matter what kind of altar you have, you will probably want to consider a few practical issues when you create it. An altar should suit your personal practice and also your realistic needs and limitations (if you hate to clean, for instance, don't have an altar with lots of fiddly little bits and pieces that will need constant dusting). It should suit your tastes rather than conforming to someone else's ideas for the proper way to construct an altar. And no matter what else it does, it should, in the end, make you happy.

After all, your altar is the center of your spiritual practice—the heart-beat of your home. Make sure that it sings to you and reflects your own magickal inner self, and don't be afraid to change things around until it feels just right. If you look at your altar and your heart rejoices, you'll know it is the perfect one for you.

Spiritual Cleaning: Not Just for Spring Anymore

I do spring cleaning just like most folks: airing out the house after a long winter of having the windows shut, clearing the stagnant energy, sweeping up the dust cougars from underneath the furniture. (I used to have dust bunnies, but the dust cougars ate them.) But I put a lot more energy—both practical and magickal—into my fall cleaning.

Yes, you read that right—I said FALL cleaning. I know we usually talk about spring cleaning; in fact, I have written articles and given classes that focus on what I call "spiritual spring cleaning." But in the last few years, I find that I am more likely to do my big cleaning and clearing push in the fall instead.

There are a couple of reasons for this. For one thing, here in the cold and snowy Northeast, we tend to get stuck in our houses a lot during the winter. (There are people who actually go outside for such winter sports as skiing and skating. Please see "cold and snowy" above for why I'm not one of them.) If I am going to spend all that time in my house, I like it to be clean and neat and have good energy.

It also seems to me that clearing, cleansing, and protection work fit well with the waning energies of the season. In the fall, things are slow-ing down. The nights are longer and the days shorter; there is less light.

All around us, the natural world is dying off or getting ready to slow or cease production—leaves fall from the trees, gardens get put to bed, birds fly south for the winter. This makes it a good time to make your own nest ready for the quieter, darker, colder months to come.

I like to start by clearing away clutter. Each of us has a different definition of clutter, of course, and I'm not suggesting that you toss your collection of vintage bottle caps if you have a deep emotional attachment to it. I'm talking about the accumulation of useless stuff that most of us have lying around—things we meant to sort through and throw away but never got around to. Old paperwork, letters and cards from people you don't even remember, clothes you never wear, tools you never use—you know what I mean. Start by doing a clear-out. Throw things away, donate them to the needy, recycle, or find a friend who will actually use whatever it is.

Once you've cleared out the clutter and organized whatever remains, then it is time to do the big fall clean and cleanse. If you want, you can start with yourself. Take a ritual bath or shower and wash away the busy, hectic summer season that lies behind us. Maybe do a fast for a day or take a couple of days to just eat really healthy to prepare your body for the tougher winter months. Fall is the perfect time to do this; since there is such an abundance of wonderful fresh fruits and veggies, you can eat healthy with virtually no effort at all.

Then clean and cleanse your house. I recently took a good look at my broom (my regular cleaning one, not my magickal one) and realized that it was over ten years old and falling apart. So the first thing I did was to buy a new broom and consecrate it for cleansing work. Then I went through the house from top to bottom and swept every room, being mindful of not just sweeping away dirt but negative or stagnant energy as well. I finished up by going through the entire place with a sage smudge stick and a salt and water mixture, clearing and cleansing all the places (like windows and doors) where energy can come and go.

Fall is also the time I do my yearly protection work on my house. I make up a mixture of sea salt, peppermint, sage, rosemary, garlic (just a token amount if I'm using it inside), and a pinch of cayenne pepper. This year, I added some charcoal from the Midsummer bonfire for an extra boost, as well as some magickal protection oil I'd made up previously. You can add anything else you like that is protective in nature. I go around the outside of the house, paying special attention to doorways, and then I go around the edges of my property. I ask that the house and those who live there be protected from anything harmful, whether intentional or accidental, and I focus all my energy on placing the house and property within a protective bubble. If you are in an apartment (or a neighborhood full of nosy people), you can always do this inside instead of outside. Don't forget your mailbox, since lots of things come into your house that way. (Fireplaces, too.)

When I'm done, the house is neater, the energy clearer, and I feel ready to settle in to my "inside" time of year, without the baggage left over from the previous, more active seasons. Of course, come spring, I'll do another cleansing to prepare for that energy, but for now I can sit on the couch with a cat (or three), a mug of mulled cider, and a good book. Who could ask for more?

Daily Household Rituals: Cleansing, Grounding, and Protection

Most of us struggle to find the time to practice our Craft the way we truly want to. It is easy for our spiritual life to get swallowed up by our mundane one, just like my dust cougars ate my dust bunnies. Luckily, there are lots of simple, easy, and fast ways to integrate our magickal practice into the things we have to do everyday anyway, like cooking, cleaning, and other mundane chores.

There are a few books out there that are designed to help you do just that (besides my book The Goddess Is in the Details, of course). I've listed some of my favorites later on. Keep in mind that some of these books only have sections devoted to small everyday magickal work—but they're all very cool and useful regardless.

Cleansing

I like to keep a few basics on hand, which makes it a lot easier to add a witchy element to cleaning or cooking or whatever else you're doing. The easiest way to do that is with herbs, many of which are readily available, inexpensive, and can be used for any number of different applications. (There are lots of rare and expensive herbs too, of course, but I see no reason to use them when there are alternatives that are just as good and leave me a few dollars to buy chocolate with.)

Most of the books I list at the end of this book will give you great suggestions for herbs and their uses, so I won't get into that here. Just keep in mind that many of your favorite herbs can be used alone or in combination with other magickal ingredients and be turned into easy-to-grab washes, sprays, cleaners, and more.

I like to make up herbal combos for a few basic purposes, such as a protection and cleansing mix. To make the base mixture, combine nine parts water and one part alcohol (cheap vodka works well), then add a few drops of each essential oil you're using. Or if you want a magickal oil for ritual use, you can put the herbs into a base oil such as olive or sesame.

In the case of the protection/cleansing mixture, I usually use geranium, rosemary, lemon, and sage. If you don't have essential oils, you can soak dried herbs in the water and alcohol; just be aware that it won't last as long as the oils would. (And you will probably want to strain out the herbs after a few days of soaking.) Store in a glass jar or bottle.

For extra oomph, you can set out the mixture under the full moon, bless and consecrate it on your altar, or draw magickal symbols on the bottle. Always make sure you label it so you know what it is later!

Once you've made up your base mixture, there are many simple and easy ways to integrate its use into your regular routines or add a new magickal boost to your everyday life.

- Put some of your magickal mix into a spray bottle (just add more water and alcohol) and use it as a room spray. The protection mix is great for this, but you might also want one for peace (for those hectic days) or love or prosperity (what household couldn't use more of those?).

- When you're cleaning, put a few drops of protection/cleansing mix on your broom or dust mop. Don't forget to focus on your goal of cleaning on a spiritual level, too.

- Add a bit to your sponge while you're cleaning, and say the following: *Clean and clear, cleanse and bless, as I wipe away this mess.*

- Or put a few drops onto a dust cloth or Swiffer wand, and wave it through the air before starting your cleaning while saying: *Water wash clean, air blow clear, fire and earth protect what's dear.* Then visualize all the areas you clean being protected as you go.

- If you are using dried herbs, you can crush up a small amount with some baking soda and sprinkle it on your carpet before vacuuming. (Peppermint and lavender are especially nice for this, but use whatever smells good to you and/or has the magickal qualities you need at the moment.) As you vacuum, visualize your magickal powder pulling all the negative energy out of the carpet.

- Lemon juice can be used to clean windows or mirrors. Just mix a few drops with some water, swirl three times clockwise with your athame or index finger, and add a magickal boost to your physical cleaning.

- I wrote an entire book about broom magick (*The Witch's Broom*), and you can find all sorts of useful hints there, but the easiest way to make sweeping a magickal activity is to bless and consecrate your everyday broom. That way, every time you use it, there is a little bit of magickal power integrated into that simple action. Of course, visualizing the broom sweeping up negativity gives it that extra oomph, too.

- Try making cleaning fun. (No, really.) My editor Elysia told me about a tarot cleaning game she created where each of the suits represents a different room to be cleaned. You can do something like that with your own deck, if you have one, or simply write down all your regular cleaning tasks on little pieces of paper and toss them into a cauldron. Pull out one piece of paper every day and work on that task for ten minutes. You'll be amazed by how fast the time goes by and how much you can get done.

- Put on some beautiful chants or fun, inspirational Pagan music to cheer you along while you clean.

Cleansing isn't just for your home, either. It is easy to add a few drops of your base mixture to a bath, along with some sea salt for extra power.

Or when you take your daily shower, give it a magickal boost by making up a simple salt scrub by combining sea salt and whichever dried herbs or essential oil you prefer. Keep it near the shower and scoop up a bit when you get under the water. As you scrub gently, visualize all your stresses and negativity being pulled out of your body and flowing down the drain. If you want, you can say "stress and strain go down the drain" a few times while doing it.

Another easy way to make your shower magickal is to chant while you're under the water. Lots of people sing in the shower, but if I am feeling the need to get in touch with my witchy side or wash away a particularly unpleasant day, I'll sing one of my favorite simple chants instead. You'll be surprised by how powerful that can be!

Keep in mind that many commercially produced cleaning products are toxic, and bad for both people and the environment. What's more, you don't need something poisonous to get things clean. Baking soda and vinegar will clean a surprising amount of surfaces in your home, including windows, sinks, tubs, and more.

Grounding, Clarity, and Peace

The previous shower suggestion also works well for doing some daily grounding. It can be tough to keep ourselves grounded in the midst of our hectic lives or find clarity when we're racing around like crazy just trying to keep up with our neverending to-do lists.

Here are a few simple things you can try. Remember to focus on your goal, whether it is grounding and centering, reaching for a moment of peace and serenity, or just looking for clarity in a confusing world.

- If you are in need of clarity, look into the nearest mirror and say, "Mirror, mirror, shining bright, bring more clarity to my sight."

- Keep a rosemary plant on a shelf or windowsill that gets bright light (if it is in the kitchen, that makes it easy to use for cooking, too). When you need a bit of clarity, break off a piece and smell it.

- For clarity, peace, or grounding, nothing beats a sage smudge stick. It only takes a moment's time to light a smudge wand and waft the sweet smoke from head to toe. It helps to clear away negativity and bring you back to a peaceful center. The more you do it, the more the scent becomes a signal. Blue Moon Circle starts every ritual by passing around a sage wand, and after all this time, just a whiff is enough to make me feel better.

- Nothing grounds better than the earth under your feet. If you can, go outside and walk barefoot on the dirt. If you can't, simply stand in the middle of the floor and close your eyes. Visualize the energy of the earth below working its way up through the layers of building and flooring between you. Reach your own energy down and grab that strong, solid earth energy, feeling it making you more solid, more grounded, more centered. (This can be done while sitting, too, if you'd rather.)

- You know that saying "stop and smell the roses"? You don't have to have a rosebush, but taking a moment to appreciate the natural world—whether it is a beautiful flower in a vase or a bird outside the window or even your cat or dog curled up at your feet—can be very grounding. Pet an animal; you'll feel better.

- For a fast and easy "emergency" grounding, mix a tiny bit of salt and water in your hand (regular table salt will do if that is all you have) and dab a bit in the middle of your forehead (your third eye) and on your lips, your chest, and your abdomen. Take a deep breath.

- If you are feeling tense or flustered, try running your hands under the water in the sink (this works away from home, too) and asking the element of water to help wash away whatever is bothering you.

- Alternately, for clarity, you can call on the element of air. Close your eyes briefly and visualize the crown chakra (on the top of your head) opening up to wisdom and clarity from above. Take a few slow, deep breaths and breathe in calm and clarity.

- When cooking, add herbs for clarity or peace to the food you are preparing.

Work on the balance in your home, too. Do a little research on feng shui; sometimes a simple shift of furnishings will also shift the energy around. Check to see if all four elements are represented more or less equally—you can add some nice rocks to get some extra earth energy or a small fountain if you need more water. Wind chimes or a dreamcatcher with feathers on the bottom can add a touch of air to a room, while candles (even if not lit) can help to bring in the essence of fire.

Tess Whitehurst's book *Magical Housekeeping* covers the topics of feng shui, cleaning, and more. It's a great place to start if you want to take this further.

Protection

It is good to occasionally do some major protection work. As you've seen, I like to integrate mine into my yearly fall cleaning. But for the more day-to-day magickal issues, there are lots of fast and easy ways to add a bit of protective magick here and there. If you only have a few minutes, you can do one of the following:

- Draw a pentacle (or protective runes) in the steam on your bathroom mirror or window after your shower. If you want, ask the gods to watch over your home.

- Sprinkle a bit of salt on your windowsills and doors (if you don't want to clean up the salt afterward, you can make a mixture of salt and water).

- Write a protection charm on a scrap of paper and tuck it into the soil of a potted plant.

- When you're getting ready to leave the house, look in the mirror first and trace a pentacle on your forehead or over your heart (you can use a bit of water if you are standing at the bathroom mirror, but otherwise, just your finger will do).

- Hang a protection charm bag by your door or make an old-fashioned charm by tying together five iron nails into the shape of a pentacle. Touch the charm as you come in or out of the house. (If you can't find iron nails, you can use bits of willow twig or whatever else appeals to you.)

- Sprinkle some salt (or salt and water) toward the back of your mailbox to ward off bad news.

- It is traditional to bury a Witch bottle under the front step of your house. They're easy enough to make: put some protective herbs, a couple of pins, maybe a clove or two of garlic, some salt or soil, and a penny or piece of red jasper into a small glass container, and place it in a hole where people will be crossing your threshold.

I have one under a brick in the walk leading to my back door (which is where everyone enters a house in the country). But if you can't do that (for instance, because you live in a tenth-floor apartment), simply draw a pentacle or the protective runes of your choice on the backside of your welcome mat.

- To protect a child, open a seam in a favorite toy or pillow, tuck a protection charm inside, then sew it shut again. (Your charm can be written on a piece of paper…it doesn't have to be large and bulky.) Try something like this: *Keep this child safe from harm with this magick and love-filled charm.*

- To add an extra air of protection to a particular room, you can place a few drops of your protection mix in some water in a diffuser.

- Add a pinch of some protective herb (or garlic) to the food you cook. You can always say something as you do so, although it isn't necessary to say it out loud if there are others around. Keep it simple, like: *I cook this food with love and affection; for those I serve, I ask protection.*

- If you'd like a helping hand, you can try leaving little gifts for the faeries or the elemental spirits. These don't have to be anything fancy—a few flower blossoms, a bit of honey in a tiny cup, a pretty shell or stone.

We tend to think of magickal work as something apart from the rest of our lives—something we can only do if we set aside an hour or find a room where no one else will be. In truth, most of the Witches throughout history probably did much of their magick on the fly—mixing it into the food they cooked, the cloth they wove, and floors they swept. There's no reason that we as modern Witches can't do the same. Use your imagination. The sky's the limit!

The Magickal Car

Don't forget your car while you are doing all this magickal work. For many of us, our vehicles are like an extension of our homes (especially if you have a long commute to work and need to decompress). Here are a few quick suggestions for ways to add a little magick to your car, truck, van, or motorcycle.

- Do the same kind of cleansing and protection work on your car as you would do on your home. Add cleansing or protective herbs to the bucket when you clean it, or spritz it with a little protection spray. Clear the energy with a sage smudge stick every once in a while, particularly if people have been arguing inside the car or if you have had an accident or close call.

- Draw a pentacle or protection runes on the backside of the floor mats, add some protection mix to your wash water when you're cleaning the car, or bless and consecrate the wax you use before you rub it into the car (if you visualize the wax as a shield of protection as you're rubbing it in, that will make it even more powerful).

- Hang a charm or witchy ornament from the rearview mirror.

- Slap on a bumper sticker that proudly proclaims your magickal nature. A couple of my favorites include "My Other Car Is a Broom" and "Things Haven't Been the Same Since They Dropped That House on My Sister." Of course, Magic the Cat is particularly partial to "The Goddess Is Alive and Magick Is Afoot!" (Here's a helpful hint: not only does AzureGreen.com have a huge assortment of great bumper stickers from the silly to the spiritual, but they also sell magnetic backing you can put your stickers on so you can remove them from the car when going someplace they might get you into trouble—your Christian in-laws' house for Sunday dinner, for instance.)

- Instead of listening to pop songs while you drive, change things up and sing along to a DVD of chants or Pagan songs, or listen to an audio book by one of your favorite witchy authors (fiction or nonfiction).

- Draw or paint protective runes in places they can't be easily seen—you'll still know they're there.

- Place a protection charm or prayer in the glove compartment.

- When you need to get away, even for just an hour or two, drive along someplace where the scenery out the window is beautiful. Your car can be your broomstick, transporting you to someplace magickal.

Five-Minute Earth Protection and Reconnection Ritual
MELANIE MARQUIS

Even on a busy day, I can usually find five minutes or so to spare for a bit of magick. In fact, I need it; when I don't take time for magick and ritual, I feel myself sliding down in the dumps, and quick. Here's an easy five-minute ritual I do each day to help me reconnect to the earth while offering my own magickal power toward the protection of that earth.

The ritual starts when I head outside. I pick up a rock or simply touch a tree, a leaf, a flower, or the bare ground. I feel the powerful earth energies course through my hand and into the rest of my body. I let this energy flow through me, and I add to it my own feelings of love and passionate attachment for the earth. Once this power seems super magnified, I take a good look at the landscape surrounding me, then I close my eyes and envision other landscapes in the world that could use some magickal protection. I might focus on the seas, the rainforests, or a local park, depending on the needs of the day and on my intuitive inclinations.

Now that I'm thinking about both the land right around me and any land farther away that I want to protect, I conjure in my heart a feeling of great strength. I imagine someone threatening the earth, and I use my feelings of anger toward that person to project an emotion of strength, courage, and defense. I send this protective energy out through my hand and into the earth; holding my hand palm-down, with fingertips together, I trace the shape of a pentacle in mid-air horizontal with the ground, projecting through my palm as I do so as much defensive power as I can muster. I visualize an impenetrable, protective orb surrounding both my immediate area and whatever additional areas I have in mind to protect.

Next, I pick up a rock, touch the ground, or hold a leaf or a flower again, letting the earth energies flow into my body and sending back into the rock, ground, leaf, or flower my own feelings of thanks, love, and gratitude for the magick we just shared.

The ritual complete, I return to my day feeling reconnected to the natural world and much happier and centered than I did before taking the five minutes out for magick. It feels good to do even a little magick to help along our Mother Earth, and as Witches, it's only natural that we do so every chance we get!

God and Goddess
in Everyday Life

We tend to think of the God and Goddess at the sabbats, and the Goddess especially on full moon nights. But, in truth, they are always with us—not just on special days but on every day. They are with us as we wake in the morning, as we go off to work, and as we feed our families and friends, watch TV, read a book, and deal with life's blessings and adversities.

The problem, at least as I have found in my own case, is that we are often so busy living our lives, we forget they're there. Not that we think they're gone—more that we forget to think about them at all.

This isn't due to any lack of reverence or appreciation on our part, or an indication of loss of faith. It is more a symptom of the world we live in, where we are so busy running to keep up that we sometimes forget to take time to pay attention to the things that really matter: the people we love, the natural world around us, the deities we worship.

I am as guilty of this as anyone else. I sometimes have to remind myself to stop, take a deep breath, and hit the pause button long enough to go to the movies with a friend or watch the birds out the window or say a prayer.

You might say, "Why bother? I haven't been taking the time to pay attention to the gods outside of my usual practice, and I'm fine."

And you probably are. Most of us are. But we're also missing out on an important connection we could be making at least a little more often.

Think about how it feels to be in sacred space during ritual, with the moon shining down from above and that feeling of energy and focus and sheer wonder that arises when things are just right. Now think about having a touch of that magick every day.

I'm not suggesting that you walk around with your head in the clouds or ignore the necessities of real life. What I am suggesting is that you try to find a little bit of the Divine in the midst of the mundane, and allow that divine spirit to shine through you into the world you inhabit. You, and those around you, might just be the better for it.

Seeing the World Through Goddess Eyes

In general, Pagans believe in *immanence*, which basically means that the Divine is not separate from the mundane but rather manifests itself in everyday things. Instead of a god who is far removed from the human world, we see our God/dess as both outside of us and within us. While we definitely perceive deity as something greater and more powerful, many of us also believe that each human being contains a tiny spark of the Divine within.

I definitely hold that to be true. But sometimes it can be hard to see ourselves as sacred beings or come from a place of what the Buddhists call loving-kindness. We look at the world through our own somewhat limited vision and forget to call on that God and Goddess within.

I had a remarkable experience years ago that forever changed how I looked at the people around me. It reminded me that as I move through my life, I can see the world differently if I choose to look through Goddess eyes. And while I can't, unfortunately, reproduce this experience for anyone, I can share what happened to me, and maybe you will find your own way to make this connection.

Back in the days when I was battling serious chronic illness, I turned to a number of nontraditional approaches to work on regaining health and balance in my life. One of the most effective of those turned out to be hypnotherapy. Of course, it probably helped that the woman I went to was not just a PhD in alternative psychology but also a longtime practicing Witch trained in shamanic techniques. (I still work with her to this day, and she's *freaking amazing*, so not all hypnotherapy will be like mine.)

As it sometimes happens, I got a little more than I bargained for when I started doing hypnotherapy to try and figure out what processes in the back of my brain might be sabotaging my body's efforts to be well. Past-life regressions just showed up, for one thing (which kind of decided me on the subject of reincarnation once and for all, although that's not what I'd been looking for); that was pretty fascinating all by itself, since I wasn't even sure I *believed* in past lives before I started.

But more than that, there were times during the trance state when I seemed to connect with beings and spirits that I might not have been open to when I was "awake." My spirit animals first came to me during hypnotherapy (you remember the flock of sheep, right?), as did my spirit guide, a female figure named Magda who is fond of kicking my metaphorical butt when I do something stupid.

None of this has much relevance to the current discussion other than to establish the fact that for me, at least, hypnotherapy opened up some doors that might not have been opened otherwise. The trance state is an interesting thing, and its aftereffects often lingered for a while after the session was over.

One day, when I was walking around after a particularly powerful session, I found myself seized by a feeling that I can only call a manifestation of that immanence we talked about earlier. As I strolled down the street, I saw a woman sitting at a sidewalk café. By the norms of our society, she was very overweight and not particularly young or well dressed or pretty. And yet, when I looked at her, she *shone* with beauty. As I continued to stroll down the street, I realized that everyone I looked at was the same—each of them different, imperfect, flawed, and yet so very beautiful because of that. I didn't look at a man and think, as we so often do, "too tall, too skinny." I just thought "how beautiful."

And I realized that I was seeing other people as the Goddess sees us: all of us beautiful because we are as she made us. It was one of the most profound and humbling and elevating moments of my entire life.

Sadly, within an hour or so, that feeling of channeling her so intensely faded away, and I was just me again. But I never looked at the people around me the same. Yes, sometimes I forget and think in terms of what our society considers ugly or weird or unattractive. But I try to remember that moment and view each person through Goddess eyes, seeing the beauty intrinsic in every one of us.

If you want to do this, you can ask for the Goddess to grant you her vision temporarily. Who knows, maybe it will happen to you too. Even if it doesn't, you can try looking at people without judging them by the very limited standards of the culture we live in, which only sees people as attractive if they are thin, young, and have conventionally pretty features. Admire the abundant curves and beaked noses and swarthy skin; find the beauty in frizzy hair and gray hair and no hair at all.

I try to remember that somewhere within me is a little piece of Goddess and a little piece of God, and let that light shine out into the world so that I might see the light of others shining back. Give it a whirl, why don't you, and see what you think.

Strength in Times of Trouble

I don't know about you, but I have found that in times of crisis, I have a tendency to forget most of the important lessons I spent years learning (usually the hard way). Things like "panicking *never* helps a situation" or "I'll feel better and be able to cope better if I stick to a healthy diet during a crisis instead of eating so-called comfort food full of sugar and fat." (Dark chocolate doesn't count—everyone knows that's health food.)

But more than those kinds of things, I forget to use the extra tools available to me as a Witch. I can't count the number of times I've had some kind of serious issue and someone asked me, "Have you done a spell?"

That sound you hear is me smacking my forehead, usually while rolling my eyes and muttering something like, "A spell…why didn't I think of that?" But when things are blowing up or just generally getting away from me, I *don't* think of it.

I also tend to forget about the greatest tool of all: I don't ask for help. At least, not in any meaningful, focused way. (Apparently glaring at the sky and saying, "Oh, for the love of god!" doesn't actually count.)

That's right. Me, the woman who has been a practicing Witch for many years, a high priestess for over a decade, and has written umpteen books telling other people how to practice the Craft. In the middle of a crisis, I don't always remember to think like a Witch. So don't worry if sometimes you forget, too.

There are other reasons why people don't ask the gods for help, beyond just not thinking to do so. Many of us have been brought up to believe that asking for help (from anyone—friends, family, and gods included) is a sign of weakness or an indication that we have somehow failed if we couldn't solve whatever the problem is on our own. Sometimes we don't feel worthy of help—maybe that little voice in the back of our heads is saying that if a bad thing happened to us, perhaps we deserved it or did something to bring it upon ourselves.

It's not unusual to have issues you are comfortable asking for help with and others you're not. For some reason, I am perfectly happy to do prosperity magick when I need to, but I rarely did healing magick for myself until recently, despite years of dealing with health issues. It wasn't an intentional decision exactly; I think I was just so focused on my usual ways of trying to find answers, it didn't occur to me that I was missing an obvious approach.

Other people have reservations about doing any magickal work for their own benefit, although they would be happy to do it for others. Either way, there are lots of reasons why we don't ask for help, but my theory is this: *it never hurts to ask.* You won't necessarily get the help you ask for, but I believe the gods are always listening, and unless you spend all your time asking them for trivial or frivolous things, they're unlikely to mind if you ask. In fact, they may have been waiting for you to do just that.

There are, however, a couple of things to keep in mind as you pray, do spellwork, or say "please, I need help."

Make sure that when you are doing magickal work or asking for help, you really need it.

As I said before, neither prayer nor magick is appropriate for trivial things, and there are many problems that can be readily dealt with through mundane means. Magick is a tool, but it isn't the only one you have available to you. Make sure it is the right approach for whatever issue you are dealing with. (Big issues often require both magickal and mundane solutions.) Often it is a good idea to try mundane approaches first, then turn to magick if they fail to solve the problem.

Remember that Witchcraft is a religion that advocates personal responsibility.

In other words, the gods help those who help themselves. Don't do a spell or ask for help and then just sit there waiting for a miracle. You might get one, but it has been my experience that the gods are more likely to send aid when you create opportunities for them to do so.

Say you lose your job, for instance. Yes, by all means, ask the gods to send you the best possible new job for you. But then go out and do everything you can to find that job—put in applications, network, and research opportunities. The more you do, the more channels you create for that help to manifest.

Keep an open mind.

It is easy to get stuck on our own ideas of what the right answer to a crisis might be. But what we think is the answer isn't always the only good option; sometimes by being fixated on one solution, we miss others that might, in the end, be even better.

Take the "lost your job" example. You might think that the only thing you want is to get a replacement job that is the same as the one you lost. So if you do a spell or say a prayer asking the gods to give you back your old job or find you the exact same job elsewhere, you are, in essence, limiting their ability to help you.

Sometimes a crisis, a disaster, or a terrible loss is actually an opportunity for change or growth. (Although admittedly, they rarely feel like that at the time they're happening!) Try to keep an open mind about the possibilities an otherwise unpleasant or challenging situation may create. If you ask for the best possible outcome rather than something specific, perhaps the universe will send you an entirely new and unexpected career path or help from someone you might not have considered or the realization that you'd stayed at a job you hated because you thought you needed the security it provided when, in fact, there was another solution.

Sometimes the answer is no.

We can always ask for help, but sometimes the answer is no. There can be any number of reasons for that, many of which only become clear in hindsight, long after the crisis is over. (Sometimes we never understand the reasons for things. Unfortunately, that is simply a part of life.)

If the gods don't answer our prayers or if our spells don't work, that doesn't mean that we did something wrong or that the gods weren't listening. Here are a few of the reasons why you might not get the results you were hoping for:

IT CAN'T BE FIXED—Sometimes there simply is no solution. If you are praying for someone you love not to die and they die anyway, it may have just been their time. We might have been asking for the impossible, or it might be that there are other elements at play that we know nothing about.

IT SHOULDN'T BE FIXED—Sometimes the things we think we want aren't the things we should have or it isn't the right time for us to get them. If you ask for that job back but there are reasons you shouldn't have it, the gods may say, "No. Look elsewhere for your answers." Or if you beg them to save your marriage and they don't, it might be that there is someone better waiting for you down the road or that the marriage was unhealthy for the people involved. If you ask for the same thing over and over again and the answer is still no, you may need to take another look at the situation and ask yourself if there is a reason why.

THERE IS A LESSON TO BE LEARNED—Much of our lives are full of challenges and mixed blessings; that's often how we learn the most important lessons. If the same things keep happening to you over and over again (ahem, been there, done that, have the T-shirt to prove it), you might want to look at the patterns in your life and ask yourself if there is something you should be learning from them. Are you making the same mistakes? Are there behaviors or attitudes you need to change in order to produce a different outcome? Try to look at the challenges you face as opportunities to learn and grow rather than just crap life keeps throwing at you for no reason whatsoever.

YOU CAUSED THE PROBLEM AND YOU NEED TO CLEAN IT UP YOURSELF—A little bit like parents, sometimes the gods are going to look at a crisis and say something along the lines of, "Dude, you made this mess. Don't ask me to clean it up for you." If you lost that job because you mouthed off at your boss one time too many or came in drunk or didn't bother to get your work done in a timely fashion, the gods aren't likely to magickally produce another one for you. They may help you find ways to do better the next time if you ask them for help with that, but don't expect them to fix problems you created of your own free will. Even magick doesn't do that.

YOU NEED THE CRISIS TO GET YOU WHERE YOU REALLY ARE SUPPOSED TO BE—This is more than just the whole "lessons to be learned" issue. As I look back over my life, I can see a number of places where I was at a crossroads or completely stuck, and it took a major upset to set me on the path I needed to take. The worst things that ever happened to me—things that at the time I wondered if I could even survive—have led me to where I am today, and that's a pretty good place.

Even when you are dealing with the unthinkable—the loss of a loved one, a terrible health crisis, your entire life crashing and burning around you—and you feel like you have no control over any of it, you can still choose whether to let the crisis make you stronger and wiser or allow it to break you. You can keep an open mind and an open heart and try to learn whatever positive lessons you can despite the difficulties you face, and you can still ask for help.

The gods aren't just there to fix things. You can call on them in times of trouble to help you find the best possible path forward and the strength to walk it to the best of your ability. You can ask for patience and clarity, acceptance and serenity, guidance and resilience and courage.

And you always can ask them for love. They have that in abundance and are always willing to give to those who ask.

Making the Connection with Deity

Connecting with the gods is both easy and very, very difficult. Not because they aren't out there or willing to talk to us, but because the best way to reach them—and to really, truly hear them—is to be quiet. Quiet in mind, body, and spirit.

When is the last time you had an hour of that?

Yeah, that's what I thought.

It's not that the gods won't occasionally manifest whether or not you make the space for them to do so—in fact, they are quite well known historically for butting in when you least expect them. Still, if you want to make that connection, it is best to put forth a little effort so they know that they are welcome and you are listening.

Here are a few simple ways to open the door for God and Goddess:

- Create an altar for your particular deity, if you have one, or for deity in general. Make sure to keep it neat and clean, and perhaps put the occasion gift on it—fresh flowers, a pretty stone, or whatever you think your goddess or god would like.

- Do some research. If you are called to a particular god or goddess, do some reading and find out as much as you can about his or her history and mythology. If you aren't sure who you are intended to worship (if, indeed, there are any specific gods for you), this research may help you find the one that resonates. I have found that when you come across the right deity, you will feel a kind of *ping* that says "this is the one."

- Pay attention. Sometimes the gods choose you. If you keep stumbling across references to a particular god/dess, or if one shows up during a dream or meditation, or if you keep seeing signs that are associated with a particular deity, he or she may be calling your name. Answer.

- If you have a deity you follow, you may want to see if there are particular times of the day or month when he or she likes to be contacted (dawn for the goddess Aurora, for instance, or the dark moon for a goddess like Hecate).

- Make sure you leave a little quiet time in your life to talk to the gods. This can be first thing in the morning, before everyone else in the house is awake, or last thing at night. You can take a walk at lunchtime and empty your mind. Of course, meditation and prayer are always good too.

A FIVE-MINUTE RITUAL TO CONNECT WITH DEITY

You don't have to do this every day, but try to find five minutes at least once a week for this important task.

Sit comfortably someplace where you won't be disturbed. If you want, you can burn some sage or light some incense, but it isn't necessary. Close your eyes and let go of your day, of the now, of whatever is going on with your life. Be completely present in the moment, as much as you can (but don't worry if you don't do it perfectly—there is no wrong way to do this). Breathe in and out slowly; feel the energy and clarity from the sky above and the strength of the earth below. When you are ready, picture your deity or simply think I *am here. I am waiting. I am open. I am listening.* And see if your god or goddess has anything to say to you. If something comes up, pay attention to it, even if it doesn't make sense at the moment. You may simply feel a sense of peace or love or acceptance. That is deity, too. When you're done, say thank you and open your eyes.

If you got an image or a message, you may want to write it down in a journal or your Book of Shadows.

Looking Inside to See the God/dess in Us All

Everyone has a different idea of what deity is. Some see God and Goddess as unlimited power. Others see them as wisdom and all-encompassing knowledge. You might view them as the overarching manifestation of the natural world, or the universe, if you will, wearing a face that we can understand.

I see them as all those things and more. For me, deity is a concept so large it is not truly possible for me to really comprehend it at all—I am well aware that what I think of as God/dess is probably merely a fraction of all that they are. But mostly when I think of deity, I think of love.

That long-ago Samhain when I stood in a ritual circle for the very first time and felt the touch of God and Goddess like the clear, vibrant sound of a ringing bell in the silent darkness, that is what I felt: love, compassion, acceptance. Complete and unwavering, without hesitation or limits. It was as if she/he stood in front of me and said, "I see you. I *truly* see you. And all that I see is good."

For many of us, this is not something we have often experienced in the rest of our lives. If you are one of the lucky ones, you have someone (a parent, a friend, a significant other) who loves you unconditionally, no matter what you do or say or how often you screw up. And let's face it, we all screw up. But sadly, lots of people never experience unconditional love at all.

And this is one of the ways in which I believe we can channel that tiny spark of the Divine that lives inside each of us.

By all means, pass along what wisdom you have gathered; help those who need it when it is within your power to do so. These, too, are ways to share the essence of God/dess within. But even if you don't feel like you have any knowledge worth sharing (although you probably do), or you don't have the energy or the means to help others, you always have love to share. Always. There are no limits to the amount of love we each carry inside ourselves, and, in fact, the more we give, the more we have to give.

As you move through your life, remember that spark of divinity you hold, and do what you can to spread it around. Do your best to accept those around you as they are and love them anyway. (Even if you have to do it from several states away to preserve your sanity. Unconditional love and acceptance of who someone is *does not mean* letting people take advantage of you or abuse you; it just means understanding that people are who they are, and loving them anyway.)

And once or twice a day, when you have a moment (even if it *is* just one moment), open up your heart to the gods and let that love encompass you, too. Give yourself a hug or look in the mirror and say, "I love and accept myself just the way I am."

The renowned astronomer Carl Sagan once said, "We are made of star stuff," and it is true. The same elements that make up the stars are also inside us. We are a part of a huge, amazing universe—a tiny speck of magick amidst a world full of marvels. So every once in a while, take the time to look at the stars and remember that you have star stuff (and Goddess stuff and God stuff) inside you. How can you not love that?

Why I'm an Anglo-Saxon Pagan
ALARIC ALBERTSSON

Why do I follow an Anglo-Saxon path? There is no single, short answer to this. I do have considerable English ancestry, and I suppose that I get a little extra kick from knowing that I am following in the path of my fore-bears, but otherwise genetics has very little to do with it. "Anglo-Saxon" is a culture, not a race. In fact, one could argue that anyone who speaks English as his or her first language is fundamentally an Anglo-Saxon.

Anglo-Saxon tradition is relatively easy for English-speaking people to understand because its concepts are embedded in our language and in the cultural tales that have been passed down to us. As children, we were taught how to interact with the spirit world. English fairy tales taught us that knowing or guessing the name of a spirit gives us power over it. We know that an inappropriate gift (such as the clothing that the shoemaker gave to his elves) may drive benevolent spirits away. The gods themselves march in a divine procession through our English names for the days of the week: Tiw's-Day, Woden's-Day, Thunor's-Day, Frige's-Day. Anglo-Saxon tradition flows through our speech.

This is a convenience, but it really is not why I chose this path. To ask why I am an Anglo-Saxon Pagan is like asking why I fell in love or why I chose to pursue a writing career. Like so much in our lives, it was a merry, magical sequence of events that led me to my path. The Anglo-Saxon gods and goddesses were the first (non-Abrahamic) deities that I interacted with. Oh, sure, I was exposed to the Greek pantheon in high school, but those deities were presented as literature, not as a source of spiritual fulfillment.

Later, of course, as I met more people and become more immersed in our contemporary Pagan communities, I became familiar with the gods of many cultures: Welsh, Irish, Egyptian, Roman, Babylonian. But I kept circling back, like a moth to flame, to the gods and goddesses of the early English. Those were the gods who spoke to me.

I have been asked why I don't take a more eclectic, shotgun approach to spirituality. There is an assumption that I'm missing out on something just because I don't mix cultures in either my spiritual practice or my magical practice. But by staying true to an Anglo-Saxon path, I believe that I am learning more about Anglo-Saxon spirituality and magic than I would if I skipped around from one culture to another. This doesn't mean that I cannot participate in an Egyptian or Celtic or Wiccan ritual. My own work and worship is Anglo-Saxon, but that does not limit me in any way; it focuses me.

Moving Forward:
Lessons Along the Way

We all walk different paths through life—as Witches, as Pagans, as human beings. We don't even necessarily agree on the point of walking that path in the first place. Some people would tell you that life is simply about surviving the journey: doing whatever it takes to get through the day, the week, the year; putting one foot in front of the other until you're done. Others might say that it is about winning: being the best, making the most money, having the most to show for your journey once you're done.

There's nothing wrong with either of those approaches, and all of us need to do what we can to endure life's challenges and, if possible, reach for some kind of goals, whether they are economic, personal, or spiritual.

For me, though, the path is also about what we can learn along the way. We start out our lives as empty as a bowl, knowing only those things our instincts tell us, like crying if we are hungry, cold, or afraid. As we move through our journeys, we learn about what it is to be human, filling our bowls with the fruits of our experiences—all the knowledge we have gathered along the way.

A spiritual path helps us to integrate that knowledge into lessons that can help us make choices further down the path, and those choices mold us into the people we become. Many of the Witches and Pagans I have met along my own journey share my goal: to become the best human being I can be—the best *me* I can manage.

For me, this is the main point of following this twisted path I call my life: to learn, to grow, to be the best I can be both for myself and for the others I meet along the way. Needless to say, I am a long way from reaching that goal. I am flawed and imperfect, and I make plenty of mistakes, just like everyone else. I rarely live up to my own ideals for how I should behave or react. But my journey isn't over yet, thankfully, and so I can keep walking my path and practicing until I get it right, or at least get it better.

In the meanwhile, however, there are a few basics I have learned on the part of the journey I've taken so far. Some of them I've learned from being a Witch and a Pagan. Others I've learned just by surviving and striving, but I have made them a part of both my mundane and my magickal life. I suspect the gods have had a hand in many of the lessons, and I hope they haven't grown too frustrated with how slow a learner I am and how many times I have to be shown The Same Damned Thing before I finally figure it out.

It isn't enough simply to dance under the full moon and celebrate the sabbats with feasting and merriment or reverence and mirth. (Although these are darned good places to start.) You need to figure out what you're learning along the way, and fill your bowl to the brim with knowledge and experience and maybe even a little faith—and, if possible, share these things with others. Here's a few of the most important things I've learned. Feel free to take them out of my bowl and put them into yours.

Cultivating a Positive Attitude

Most of life is out of our control. Stuff happens on a regular basis, and some of it is wonderful; much of it, not so much.

We can rarely control the people around us or how they treat us. Although to some extent we have a choice about who we allow to be in our lives, even that is sometimes not up to us. We don't get to pick our families, after all, or our in-laws, or who our children turn out to be when they grow up.

And then there are health issues, economic issues, and oy, don't get me started on politics. Suffice it to say that while we do our best to make the world we live in a pleasant one, sooner or later, crap is going to happen. For some folks it seems like crap happens all the time *and* brings its younger brother and a few cousins along for the ride.

Life can be *hard*. And cruel and unfair. And we can't control any of that.

What we can control, however, is how we deal with the things that life throws at us.

This is what I have learned: *attitude is everything*.

You might be thinking, "Well, that's easy for you to say." But actually, it was something that took me a long, hard road to learn. I spent the first thirty-something years of my life with a lousy attitude. I was depressed and gloomy and negative. There were some good reasons for some of it; the rest of it just became part of who I was. I was still me, the same me I am now— just a pretty depressed and negative version.

And then I got sick. Not a little sick but chronic, horrible, beat-you-down sick. I felt horrible all the time, and I'm fairly certain that if you ask the folks who knew me then, they would tell you I wasn't much fun to be around. Not just because I was sick and couldn't do anything, but because I had a dark cloud over my head all the time.

Then one day I hit rock bottom, and as sometimes happens when you're lying there on the bottom, looking up at everything else, I had a realization that changed the course of the rest of my life. I realized that there was nothing I could do about being sick. For the moment, at least, I had done everything that I or any of my doctors knew how to do, and there was a very good likelihood that I was going to be sick for the rest of my life.

So I had two choices. I could be sick and miserable or I could be sick and not miserable. That was it. Those were my only two options. But they were under my control.

It turned out that having a positive attitude made a big difference in my path to better health, which was a nice bonus. (And yes, I think the gods probably sent me that illness to help me learn this important lesson.) But mostly, my life is better in general; I'm happier, I have more friends, and frankly, all that crap (and believe me, there is still crap) is easier to deal with if I choose to laugh at it instead of cry.

So this is lesson number one: a positive attitude beats a negative attitude every single time. And you get to choose which one you're going to have—that much of life, at least, is under your control. You may have to ask the gods to help you change your attitude, but even that is a choice.

NOTE: Clinical depression often requires professional intervention as well. You don't have to make an either/or decision—use all the tools you have available, whether spiritual or medical.

Appreciating What We Have Even When It Isn't Everything We Want

Right after attitude comes appreciation. Very few of us have perfect lives. Hardly anyone gets everything they want. Maybe you have a good job but no significant other. Maybe you have someone to love you but you are constantly worrying about money. Nobody has it all.

Here, again, there are two choices. You can spend lots of time and energy bemoaning the fact that you don't have everything you want or you can appreciate what you *do* have, and focus on the positive, not the negative. As Witches, we talk a lot about focus; how you focus your mental energy is important, too. Glass half full is a whole lot healthier and happier than glass half empty. Most of the time, I'm just grateful I have a glass!

Cultivating an attitude of appreciation is part of our spiritual journey. Some of it is learning to want less—figuring out what in life is truly important (here's a hint: it isn't the next fancy gadget or an expensive new outfit). Some of it is realizing that no matter how little you feel like you have, there is always someone with less.

Look at it this way: if the gods give you a gift, they are going to want you to say thank you and be grateful instead of complaining that you didn't get exactly what you wanted. And just as having a positive attitude makes your journey through life easier, having appreciation for the gifts we've been given makes life that much sweeter.

Listening to Inner Wisdom

But you don't have to listen to me; the best advice comes from within.

We all have that quiet voice inside that knows which answers are right for us. Maybe that voice comes from our own personal connection to deity—that spark within us that is God and Goddess. Maybe it is the result of what we have each learned as we walk along our path.

Either way, the trick is to *listen*. That voice can be hard to hear over the hustle and bustle of daily life. That's one of the reasons we do ritual or meditate or pray: all these things help open us up to the inner wisdom that can otherwise get lost amid the rest of the noise.

You know what is right for you. All you have to do is listen to your own inner wisdom, and then do your best to follow the path it sets you on.

The One Important Rule

There is always debate over whether or not Witchcraft has rules, and if so, what they are. That's a subject for a different book, and another one of those choices you have to make for yourself. Even the most basic rule, the Wiccan Rede, which I generally try to follow, can be a bit tricky.

At its simplest (and there are many longer, more complicated versions), the Wiccan Rede says *an it harm none, do as ye will.*

Although couched in slightly archaic language, the message is clear: do whatever you want as long as you don't hurt anyone in the process.

The problem here is that "harm none" can mean a lot of things, depending on how you look at it. For one thing, the word *none* includes your own self. So if you are following the rule, you never do anything that might hurt you. Please back away from that bag of chocolate chip cookies right now.

In addition, it can be hard to predict what will hurt someone else, either now or at some time in the future. Who among us hasn't done something with the best of intentions, only to discover that we hurt someone's feelings inadvertently or made a situation worse instead of better?

More than that, how does "harm none" apply to people who are trying to harm you? Some Witches believe in hexing; others don't. One well-known Witch, the lovely and talented Z Budapest, is famous for working with other women to hex rapists when the police have been unable to bring them to justice by conventional means. I have mixed feelings about this, since I normally am not a pro-hex Witch. Is it revenge? If so, I'm probably not in favor, since I believe the gods will deal with retribution themselves. Is it done to defend other women? Frankly, if there is no doubt who the rapist is (and that's where these things can get tricky), it is hard for me not to approve. As with the rest, how you interpret "harm none" is up to you.

A longer version of the Wiccan Rede adds the phrase "lest in thy self-defense it be, ever mind the Law of Three." That tends to be more along the lines of how I view it.

I do, in fact, try to live my life by the rules of the Wiccan Rede. But I've decided that there is one rule even more important—and a whole lot less confusing—than that one, or any of the other witchy or Pagan rules out there. More than that, I believe in my heart that this is the rule the God and Goddess most want us to follow.

What is it?

BE KIND.

I told you it was simple.

The most straightforward and basic way to channel the gods and our own inner divinity is to be kind. Kind to others (even when they are not kind to us). Kind to ourselves, although that can be even tougher. Kind to animals, both wild and domesticated. Kind to Mother Nature, who has given us this lovely planet to live on and provides us with sustenance every day.

It costs you nothing. It takes very little time and effort. And the returns can be amazing, although there is never any guarantee that you will get anything back at all. Spiritually, it is one of the most essential treasures you will find along the path. To give and receive kindness. To give and receive love.

So that's my one big rule: be kind. Smile at people you don't know, for no particular reason. Say something nice to the person at the checkout counter at the grocery store or the waiter who brings your dinner. Tell someone they look beautiful. Spread happiness. Practice acts of random kindness.

Most of all, remember to be kind to yourself. For many of us, that is a much more difficult task than being kind to others.

Forgive yourself for being an imperfect human being. The Goddess doesn't expect perfection, although she *does* expect you to try and do better. Allow yourself to be happy. Live the life you want, and follow the path of your heart.

Which brings us back around to where we started: walking the path of the everyday Witch. If this is the path you choose, if this is the one your heart wants, then give yourself permission to follow it. *Make the time*, even if it is just five minutes a day, because your spiritual path is important and because you're worth it.

After all, you have a piece of the Divine inside you, don't you? And you are made of star stuff.

So be your best self; live your best, happiest, most fulfilled life; and walk your path with grace and wisdom, with occasional stops along the way to dance with joy.

Recommended Books
for the Basics and Beyond

There are many wonderful books on Witchcraft, Wicca, and Paganism. In fact, at the end of this one you will find a list of many of my favorites…and it is a really long list. But there are some books I find myself recommending to others time after time. A few of them are classics in the witchy world, while others are by new authors with interesting and original approaches to the way we practice.

Some of them explore the basics, and others delve so deeply I found I had to read them one chapter at a time, then stop and think for a while before moving on to the next. One is an encyclopedia, while another is a collection of "magickal morsels" from many of the elders of our spiritual path recounting tales of their own journeys.

What these books have in common—and the reason I have included them in this list of recommended reading—is that they are all books I have found myself passing on to others often. Some of them I liked so much, I had everyone in Blue Moon Circle read them so we could discuss the contents or use them in our own magickal work. Some I believe represent something so elemental about the study and understanding of magick and our history as a Neopagan people that they should be required reading for everyone who is serious about their Craft. If you looked at my copies, you'd see lots of bookmarks and scraps of paper marking the sections I want to be sure to go back and reread or point out to one of my Pagan friends.

Not all of these books will appeal to every reader, and that's okay. You don't *have* to read them; there won't be a quiz. But if you are interested in expanding your knowledge and finding new ways to add depth to your practice, there are books on this list that will help you do that. And, of course, some of them are just plain fun, too. Many of these authors are among my favorites in the Pagan world, and you will find other of their books on the longer list (and a few of them kindly consented to add a few words to this book), so perhaps you will find a new favorite here, too.

It has been said that reading my books is like sitting down at the kitchen table with your friendly neighborhood high priestess for a cup of tea and a chat. So let's pretend that you are sitting across that table from me, and you ask me, "What should I read next, Deborah?"

The Basics

People often ask me either which books to start with or which ones are "required reading" for serious Witches. Those books are the ones on this list. (In alphabetical order by author, since it would be impossible to recommend one over another.)

1: Scott Cunningham, *Wicca: A Guide for the Solitary Practitioner*

If you have been involved with modern Witchcraft for more than fifteen minutes, you have probably heard of Scott Cunningham. An amazingly prolific writer, Cunningham's more than thirty books are go-to reading for many who are new to the path and plenty who have been on it for years. I have a number of them myself—eight or nine, I think, not counting this one.

Wicca: A Guide for the Solitary Practitioner may well be the most often recommended book of any I know. It is a great starting place for anyone interested in learning about Wicca, and especially for solitaries, which make up a huge number of those who practice. A follow-up book, *Living Wicca: A Further Guide for the Solitary Practitioner*, came out in 1993.

Cunningham has a simple, clear way of explaining things, and I suspect that is one of the reasons for the continued popularity of his books. (He's also written about stones and crystals, herbs, the magickal household, and much more.) He covers the basics of a Witchcraft practice with just enough philosophy to make the work meaningful without overwhelming the reader, and at the end of *Wicca: A Guide for the Solitary Practitioner* he includes a Book of Shadows complete with invocations, recipes, an herbal grimoire, and many other basics that will serve you well along the path.

Cunningham died in 1993, but his books are still at the core of many a Witchcraft practice. If you can only get one, get this one.

2: Dorothy Morrison, *Everyday Moon Magic*

Dorothy Morrison is one of the best-known and most popular authors in the Witchcraft world, and rightfully so. Her classic *Everyday Magic* has sold over 100,000 copies, and I highly recommend that one, too. In fact, I love all of her books. But since I could only pick one for this list, I chose *Everyday Moon Magic*.

After all, for most Witches, our practice centers around the moon in all her incarnations, so it makes sense to have at least one book that focuses on lunar lore on your magickal bookshelf. This one has everything you'll need: detailed discussions about our connection to the moon, the moon phases, moon magick, zodiac information, and more, as well as plenty of practical spells and rituals for everyday needs.

As with all of Morrison's work, the book is easy to read and understand, written with the author's trademark humor, warmth, and extensive knowledge.

If you ever dance around (naked or not) under the light of the full moon, this book will help you do it with grace and flare. (And if you really want some grace and flare, visit Dorothy's latest online venture at Wicked Witch Studios, where she now showcases her beautiful handcrafted witchy accessories.)

3: Starhawk, *The Spiral Dance*

Starhawk (Miriam Simos) is one of the acknowledged elders of the modern Witchcraft movement. She is a Witch, an activist, and what she calls an ecofeminist, and she cofounded the now-famous Bay Area Reclaiming Collective. One of the people directly responsible for shaping the resurgence of goddess religion in the United States, Starhawk's *The Spiral Dance* was and is one of the seminal books of the Witchcraft world.

This is one of those books that I recommend constantly to anyone who is serious about a Witchcraft practice. It not only contains rituals, invocations, exercises, and other practical magickal work, it is also a first-person history of the rebirth of our religion, written by someone who was a midwife to the process.

I especially like the twentieth-anniversary edition. In it is not only the original introduction, but also the introduction to the tenth-anniversary edition, as well as a new introduction to this one. The author looks back at the changes in both the Pagan movement and her own beliefs and attitudes, speaking frankly of what she would have done differently and the hopes she holds for the future.

The Spiral Dance explores many of the concepts that are at the core of a Witchcraft practice: the coven, creating sacred space, the Goddess and the God, magickal symbols, raising a cone of power, trance, initiation, moon rituals, the Wheel of the Year, and Witchcraft as a goddess religion. It also talks about the process of creating a religion and includes Starhawk's commentary on her own writing, looking back on it from twenty years down the line.

This is one of my favorite books, not just because it is full of wisdom, wit, and practical explanations for many of the elements I base my own practice on, but because it gives us a glimpse into a momentous time in the history of Witchcraft.

If we want to know where we are going, we need to know where we came from. *The Spiral Dance* shows us part of where the path began and points our way to the future.

4: Marion Weinstein, *Positive Magic*

Positive Magic is another one of those Witchcraft classics. First published in 1978, it has influenced generations of Witches and Pagans. The copy I have is the 1994 reprint edition; there was another, further updated version in 2008. The author died in 2009, and her death was a great loss to the Pagan community.

The subtitle on all but the last version was *Occult Self-Help*. Weinstein wasn't talking about New Age mumbo-jumbo. She was talking about using magick as a positive tool to change your life, and, in truth, this book has changed the lives of many. She explains the basics of Witchcraft, making this a great book for beginners. But she also delves into deeper aspects of the Craft, so no matter what stage of your journey you are on, this is a fabulous book to read.

Just out of curiosity, I went to Amazon to check out what people were saying about *Positive Magic*. The two chapters people mentioned the most were probably the ones she was best known for: "The Ten-Foot Pole Department" (which aspects of modern Witchcraft to stay far away from) and "Words of Power: The Work of Self-Transformation." Either of these chapters alone is worth the price of the book. Taken together with all the wisdom that fills these pages, it is a true bargain.

The high priestess who trained me introduced me both to Weinstein's *Words of Power* and to this book; she was a great teacher. So was Weinstein, who did her best to help generations of Witches learn how to be their best possible selves.

If you can only have a few Witchcraft books on your shelves, I strongly suggest you make this one of them. And if you can only have one, make it this one.

Further Exploration, Deeper Study, and an Encyclopedia

Once you get past the basics, there is a lot of room for exploration, study, and just plain fun. Some of these books are like the one you are reading now: ways to deepen your practice and help you live your best witchy life.

Others are traditional approaches to the Craft, while some will help you to advance your learning and push yourself, if you are so inclined. These are all books I recommend, for different reasons; maybe one of them will be your new favorite, too.

5: Raymond Buckland, *Buckland's Complete Book of Witchcraft*

Raymond Buckland has been practicing the Craft since before most of us were born. He studied British Traditional Witchcraft with Gerald Gardner himself, after which Buckland brought Wicca to the United States. He's written dozens of books on Witchcraft and other related subjects, including a number on Gypsy magick, since he is of Romani descent.

Buckland's Complete Book of Witchcraft is considered to be one of the classics of modern Witchcraft. The revised edition, which came out in 2002 and which I highly recommend you get if you can, added new photographs and illustrations, a preface, an index, and a helpful workbook format that allows you to record what you've learned as you go along.

The book covers an amazing range of topics (which is only to be expected by something with "complete" in the title, I suppose), including chapters on history and philosophy, beliefs, tools, covens and rituals, the sabbats, divination, herbalism, the how-to's of practicing magick, and more.

For those who are interested in learning the more traditional forms of Wicca, there is probably no better book. Even if, like me, your practice is more eclectic, there is still much useful information to be found here. I use it as a reference book all the time.

This book represents our origins—where modern American Wicca began, the roots from which sprang many of the branches that now compose the ever-spreading tree that is Witchcraft. It is both practical and philosophical, and truly is one of the classics that belong on every Witch's shelf.

6: Raven Digitalis, *Shadow Magick Compendium*

Raven Digitalis is one of the bright new stars in the Pagan publishing world. His first book, *Goth Craft*, brought him instant acclaim, but it was his second book, *Shadow Magick Compendium*, that knocked my socks off.

The back of the book says it all:

> Too often, we suppress the shadow in our quest for illumination. But without a contrasting darkness, no light would exist at all.
>
> Raven Digitalis plunges into the shrouded half of the great spiritual balance, proving that an exploration of the shadows is not only safe but essential...

Shadow Magick Compendium is divided into five sections: The Internal Shadow, The External Shadow, The Astral Shadow, The Shadow of Nature, and The Shadow of Society. It provides a wonderful guide for walking through areas of our own darker selves that we might be uncertain about exploring.

Don't be fooled by the author's relative youth or unconventional appearance. He is a serious practitioner, the cofounder of his own magickal order, and a deep, deep thinker. *Shadow Magick Compendium* looks at magickal work from a very different angle, and if you are trying to expand your practice, that is a very good thing indeed.

7: Denise Dumars, *Be Blessed*

Be Blessed: Daily Devotions for Busy Wiccans and Pagans is my kind of book: short and sweet and filled to the brim with practical suggestions for everyday Witches. There are lots of books with daily devotions for the traditional religions, but this is one of the few for ours. And unlike the usual devotional books, which are set up as a calendar, all these little gems can be done on any day of the year. Visualization, meditations, and affirmations are just some of the elements included in this book, which is suitable for any Witch, no matter which form of the Craft he or she practices.

Be Blessed is written in an easy-to-read, conversational tone, and Dumars shares many of her own stories as a way to make her advice more accessible. Funny, warm, and sensible, this book is a treasure for every magickal collection.

CHAPTER 11

8: Judika Illes, *The Element Encyclopedia of Witchcraft*

The subtitle of this book is *The Complete A–Z for the Entire Magical World*, and believe it or not, that's not an exaggeration. At a staggering 886 pages, this amazing book covers an incredibly diverse amount of information on anything and everything related to magic and Witchcraft, with chapters on animals, books, botanicals, creative arts, the divine Witch, fairies, fairy tale Witches, food and drink, the hag, the horned one, magickal arts, magickal professions, places to travel, tools of Witchcraft, Witchcraft persecution, women's mysteries, and more.

Illes has written a number of other encyclopedias, most notably *The Element Encyclopedia of 5000 Spells*, and I own most of them, but this one is my favorite as well as the most useful. Crammed with an unbelievable range of information, facts, history, and myths, this is one of my go-to research books whether I am working on a book for Llewellyn or trying to find an interesting idea for a novel.

You could, of course, sit down and read the book from beginning to end, but I find this sort of encyclopedia is really fun to just open at random and read whatever pops up. I have never been disappointed by what I've found between its pages. It is also great if you are trying to find out something in particular about, for instance, magickal places or mythical figures.

I can't imagine how long it took Illes to accumulate all this knowledge, but luckily for us, we don't have to go out and search for it in a million different places because she has conveniently assembled it for us in one really large book.

9: Melanie Marquis, *The Witch's Bag of Tricks*

Melanie Marquis is another rising star in the Pagan community. She may be young (at least compared to us old crones), but she has already made her mark by founding the United Witches Global Coven and organizing the Denver Pagans. And then there is this book.

One of the unfortunate byproducts of many years of practice is that you can sometimes get stuck in a rut, doing the same old things the same old way all the time. In short, your magick loses its magick. It happens to the best of us eventually, unless we are very lucky.

If you're feeling that lack of a creative spark in your magickal practice, this is the book for you. Although it would be useful for Witches at any stage of their practice, it is particularly aimed at those who have been on this path for some time and need something to jumpstart their practice. Or, as it says in the subtitle, *Personalize Your Magick & Kickstart Your Craft.*

Although the book is aimed at Solitary Eclectics, Blue Moon Circle found it very useful for our group work as well. Marquis's book is full of useful suggestions for reenergizing your spellwork and rituals and increasing your power potential. The chapter called "What We and Magick Are Made Of" is worth the price of the book all by itself.

If your practice feels a little stale, you clearly need *The Witch's Bag of Tricks.*

10: Christopher Penczak, *The Mystic Foundation*

One of the complaints most often heard among those who have been following the Pagan path for some time is this: all you can find are Wicca 101 books!

That's something of an exaggeration, of course, because there are plenty of great tomes on various aspects of advanced magick, but it is true that they are much harder to find than the books written for those who are new to the path.

Even among those more advanced books, though, *The Mystic Foundation* stands out from all the others. The book explores the essence of the universe and how that affects our own lives and spiritual journeys. Penczak looks not only at Paganism, but also at the wider scope of mystic thought throughout the world, including Christianity, Islam, Druidism, and Taoism, to shine a light on the universal truths they all share.

This is *not* a lightweight read. It delves deep and makes you think. But don't let that discourage you from taking the journey. And the book isn't all theory, philosophy, and history—there are also practical exercises and rituals for dream exploration, aura cleansing, chakra balancing, speaking with spirit guides, and much, much more.

The subtitle of the book is *Understanding and Exploring the Magical Universe*. That sounds like a lot to promise, but I assure you, this book delivers.

Penczak is the founder of the Temple of Witchcraft tradition, and he has devoted many years to teaching the Craft to others. His extensive study in the areas of shamanism, Reiki healing, and the Qabalah shine through clearly in this book, and show how moving beyond the sometimes narrow boundaries of modern Witchcraft can help you create a magickal practice with wider mystical foundations.

11: Dianne Sylvan, *The Circle Within*

This is one of those books I mentioned earlier—one of the ones I liked so much, I ended up getting one for every member of Blue Moon Circle so we could read it and discuss it together. In fact, I recommend this book so often that I have two copies, so I can always have one at home and one to lend out to others.

So what is it about this small, simple book that gets me so excited? Dianne Sylvan isn't one of those authors with dozens of books and a name everyone recognizes (although they should). This book isn't on everyone's "must read" list, like *The Spiral Dance*—so why is it on mine?

Because, frankly, this is my kind of book. *The Circle Within: Creating a Wiccan Spiritual Tradition* is all about creating your own path. With topics that include cultivating an ongoing personal relationship with deity, ethics and standards of behavior, the elements of a daily practice, and more, this small tome gives you all the tools you need to move your practice of the Craft beyond what you were taught and into something personal and meaningful.

Sylvan's chapter on "Building a Practice" actually changed the way I viewed my own spiritual life, and I have referenced this book in *The Goddess Is in the Details*, as well as numerous other things I've written. *The Circle Within* is where I discovered that I didn't need to make my daily practice—and my connection with the gods—something complicated and time-consuming.

Everything in this book is simple and speaks straight to the heart. The back cover says, "Move beyond the basics and enter the sacred space of the Circle within."

Who doesn't want to do that?

12: Patricia Telesco, *Cakes and Ale for the Pagan Soul*

Raymond Buckland said about this book (from the back cover):

> This wonderful compendium of life lessons brings together the recognized pioneers of Neopaganism. All are leaders and authors in their own right, but seldom are they brought together between the covers of one book. There is so much variety here that it is impossible to encapsulate it, but suffice it to say, this book is to be owned and treasured.

I couldn't have said it better.

Editor Patricia Telesco (a fabulous witchy writer herself) brings together forty-five voices from the Pagan community—a veritable "who's who" of influential Wiccans, Witches, and Pagans, including Margot Adler, Starhawk, Dorothy Morrision, Oberon Zell-Ravenheart, Selena Fox, Ashleen O'Gaea, Phyllis Curott, Gail Wood, and many more.

They all have their own tales to tell. Some are funny, poignant, wise, or thoughtful, but all of them offer something different and valuable to the reader. I like the way Telesco describes it in her introduction:

> As you might have guessed, this isn't a how-to book per se. It's more like sitting around a campfire with more than forty people, many of whose names you have probably heard in passing somewhere. As the fire burns, each tells a story—of hope, of transformation, of love, of struggle and victory. Some choose instead to share recipes, insights, or poems. This is, in fact, our version of a bardic circle, where the songs are unique, just like the person sharing them.

So grab a copy of this book, pull up a seat next to the fire, and read about what our elders, teachers, and wisemen and wisewomen have to say. With forty-five different voices to listen to, one of them is bound to have something important to say to you.

18: Gail Wood, *The Wild God*

Gail Wood is one of the quiet voices of the modern Pagan world. She has written a few great books (including one of my other favorites, *Rituals of the Dark Moon: 13 Lunar Rites for a Magical Path*), but isn't as well known as some of the bigger-name authors. If you've never heard of her, I can tell you, you're missing out, just as you may be missing something if your Witchcraft practice focuses only on the Goddess.

Don't get me wrong—I definitely connect more strongly to a goddess figure than I do to a masculine god, and I am very grateful for a religion that allows me to make that connection. But Witchcraft is all about nature, and the duality of God and Goddess reflects the duality in all the rest of the natural world. Yet there are many more books on the Goddess and how to worship her than there are about her consort, the God.

The Wild God: Rituals and Meditations on the Sacred Masculine fills in the missing space. This book is for both men and women who are seeking to balance their spiritual practice with a deeper look at the male deity and his role in Pagan spirituality. Wood looks at the god in his role as Lover, Son, Consort, and Father, and shows us ways to connect with that male energy.

I've picked books for this list that I thought represented something important for those who are following the Pagan path in their own lives. Even those of us who left the religions we were born to (at least in part) because of a discomfort with the traditional male patriarchal god figure can benefit from this clear and simple book on how to acknowledge and tune in to the Pagan God. After all, he is one-half of the whole picture and as filled with magick and power and potential as his lady, the Goddess.

The Wild God makes it easy for both men and women to find a clearer understanding of the sacred masculine, and there are very few books that do so. Wood follows the journey the God makes over the course of a year, as well as discussing the God in general and the role of the priest in Pagan spirituality. Her instructions for both meditation and ritual are clear and easy to follow, but more than that, she shines a light on a part of our magickal path that is too often ignored. This is a small book by an independent press and can be difficult to find, but I assure you it is worth the search.

....
Book Lists

Daily Reading

Goddesses for Every Day: Exploring the Wisdom & Power of the Divine Feminine Around the World by Julie Loar (New World Library, 2008)

Living Earth Devotional: 365 Green Practices for Sacred Connection by Clea Danaan (Llewellyn, 2013)

Pagan Every Day: Finding the Extraordinary in Our Ordinary Lives by Barbara Ardinger (Red Wheel/Weiser, 2006)

The Real Witch's Year: Spells, Rituals, and Meditations for Every Day of the Year by Kate West (Element, 2004)

365 Goddesses: A Daily Guide to the Magic and Inspiration of the Goddess by Patricia Telesco (HarperOne, 1998)

Witches' Spell-A-Day Almanac: Holidays & Lore, Spells, Rituals & Meditations (published yearly by Llewellyn Worldwide)

Of course, you can draw inspiration from books about other spiritual paths, as well as thoughtful or philosophical books that aren't based on religion at all. A few classics:

Buddha's Little Instruction Book by Jack Kornfield (Bantam Books, 1994)

Every Day Is a Blessing: 365 Illuminations to Lift the Spirit by Aaron Zerah (Warner Books, 2002)

Notes to Myself: My Struggle to Become a Person by Hugh Prather (Bantam Books, 1970)

One Minute Wisdom by Anthony de Mello (Doubleday, 1985)

The Prophet by Kahlil Gibran

Tao Te Ching (I like the version by Stephen Mitchell, but there are many good ones out there)

Connecting with Goddess and God

Celtic Lore & Spellcraft of the Dark Goddess: Invoking the Morrigan by
Stephanie Woodfield (Llewellyn, 2011)

Goddess Alive! Inviting Celtic & Norse Goddesses into Your Life by Michelle
Skye (Llewellyn, 2007)

Goddess Aloud! Transforming Your World Through Rituals & Mantras by
Michelle Skye (Llewellyn, 2010)

*The Goddess Guide: Exploring the Attributes and Correspondences of the Divine
Feminine* by Priestess Brandi Auset (Llewellyn, 2009)

The Goddess Path: Myths, Invocations & Rituals by Patricia Monaghan
(Llewellyn, 1999)

*The Once & Future Goddess: A Sweeping Visual Chronicle of the Sacred
Female and Her Reemergence in the Cultural Mythology of Our Time* by
Elinor W. Gadon (HarperCollins, 1989)

These are just the tip of the iceberg—the books I happen to have read (and
own) myself. I encourage you to discover your own favorite books that
explore the identity and path of the God and Goddess in all their many
manifestations. If you find one you particularly like, share it with me.

Kitchen Magick

Bud, Blossom & Leaf: The Magical Herb Gardener's Handbook by Dorothy
Morrison (Llewellyn, 2001)

Cottage Witchery: Natural Magick for Hearth and Home by Ellen Dugan
(Llewellyn, 2005)

Cunningham's Encyclopedia of Magical Herbs by Scott Cunningham
(Llewellyn, 1985)

Cunningham's Encyclopedia of Wicca in the Kitchen by Scott Cunningham
(Llewellyn, 1990)

*The Real Witches' Kitchen: Spells, Recipes, Oils, Lotions, and Potions from the
Witches' Hearth* by Kate West (Llewellyn, 2002)

If you aren't good at creating your own recipes from scratch, try these three great witchy cookbooks (I can vouch for many of the recipes):

Cucina Aurora Kitchen Witchery: A Collection of Recipes for the Novice Kitchen Witch by Dawn M. Hunt (Dawn M. Hunt, 2010). Dawn has licensed some of her recipes and authorized sellers at various events. I picked up a couple of her magickal oils at the local Faerie Festival, and they are delicious!

The Wicca Cookbook: Recipes, Ritual, and Lore by Jamie Wood and Tara Seefeldt (Celestial Arts, 2000). Includes seasonal recipes and lots of great lore and history.

Witch in the Kitchen: Magical Cooking for All Seasons by Cait Johnson (Destiny Books, 2001). Includes instructions for creating a kitchen altar as well as seasonal dishes.

Covens

Inside a Witch's Coven by Edain McCoy (Llewellyn, 2003)

The Real Witch's Coven by Kate West (Llewellyn, 2010)

Spellworking for Covens: Magick for Two or More by Edain McCoy (Llewellyn, 2002)

Wicca Covens: How to Start and Organize Your Own by Judy Harrow (Citadel Press, 1999)

The Witch's Coven: Finding or Forming Your Own Circle by Edain McCoy (Llewellyn, 1997)

Raising Pagan Children

Circle Round: Raising Children in Goddess Traditions by Starhawk, Diane Baker, and Anne Hill (Bantam Books, 1998)

The Family Wicca: The Craft for Parents and Children by Ashleen O'Gaea (Llewellyn, 1994)

Raising Witches: Teaching the Wiccan Faith to Children by Ashleen O'Gaea (Career Press, 2002)

NOTE: Starhawk also has written a wonderful children's book called *The Last Wild Witch: An Eco-Fable for Kids and Other Free Spirits* (Mother Tongue Ink, 2009) if you are looking for a positive take on Witches to share with young children.

The Magickal Home

Cottage Witchery: Natural Magick for Hearth and Home by Ellen Dugan (Llewellyn, 2005)

Cunningham's Encyclopedia of Wicca in the Kitchen by Scott Cunningham (Llewellyn, 1990)

Everyday Magic: Spells & Rituals for Modern Living by Dorothy Morrison (Llewellyn, 1998)

The Magical Household: Empower Your Home with Love, Protection, Health, and Happiness by Scott Cunningham and David Harrison (Llewellyn, 1983)

Magical Housekeeping: Simple Charms & Practical Tips for Creating a Harmonious Home by Tess Whitehurst (Llewellyn, 2010)

Mrs. B's Guide to Household Witchery: Everyday Magic, Spells, and Recipes by Kris Bradley (Weiser Books, 2012)

To Walk a Pagan Path: Practical Spirituality for Every Day by Alaric Albertsson (Llewellyn, 2013)

My Books

If you liked this book, you may want to check out some of the others I have written. Magic the Cat particularly recommends the Everyday Witch books because she was my co-author (and she gets extra treats every time we sell one).

Circle, Coven & Grove: A Year of Magickal Practice (Llewellyn, 2007)

Everyday Witch A to Z: An Amusing, Informative, and Inspiring Guide to the Wonderful World of Witchcraft (Llewellyn, 2008)

Everyday Witch A to Z Spellbook: Wonderfully Witchy Blessings, Charms & Spells (Llewellyn, 2010)

Everyday Witch Book of Rituals: All You Need for a Magickal Year (Llewellyn, 2012)

The Goddess Is in the Details: Wisdom for the Everyday Witch (Llewellyn, 2009)

Witchcraft on a Shoestring: Practicing the Craft Without Breaking Your Budget (Llewellyn, 2010)

The Witch's Broom: The Craft, Lore & Magick of Broomsticks (Llewellyn, 2014)

Guest Authors

I am SO grateful for all the wonderful authors who graciously agreed to add their words of wisdom to mine, ensuring that you, the reader, got a wider vision of the witchy world.

After all, one of the best parts of being a Pagan and a Witch is that there are so many different approaches—so many "right" ways to look at things. That's why I asked some of my favorite authors (some of them friends, others of them simply people in the Pagan world whose opinions and writing I respect) to add their own particular input to this book.

You will find their names on one or more of the recommended reading lists, but in case you are unfamiliar with them, here is a little more about the folks who kindly shared their own wisdom.

Alaric Albertsson

Alaric is the author of several books on Paganism, including *To Walk a Pagan Path: Practical Spirituality for Every Day*. Over the past four decades, Alaric's personal spiritual practice has developed as a synthesis of Anglo-Saxon tradition, country beliefs, herbal studies, and rune lore. A native of the Midwest, he now lives in Pennsylvania.

Blake Octavian Blair

Blake Octavian Blair is an eclectic Pagan, published author, ordained minister, shamanic practitioner, Usui Reiki Master Teacher, tarot reader, and musician. Blake blends various mystical traditions from both the East and West, along with a reverence for the natural world, into his own brand of modern Neopaganism and magick. He holds a degree in English and religion from the University of Florida. Blake is a regular contributing author to Llewellyn's annuals and *The Magician*, the Tarot Guild of Australia's journal. He is an avid reader, crafter, and practicing vegetarian. Blake lives with his beloved husband, an aquarium full of fish, and an indoor jungle of houseplants. Visit him on the web at www.blakeoctavianblair.com or write him at blake@blakeoctavianblair.com.

Kris Bradley

Kris "Mrs.B." Bradley is a married mother of three and domestic housewitch. She is the author of the now retired Confessions of a Pagan Soccer Mom blog and of the book *Mrs. B.'s Guide to Household Witchery*. You can find her at her new website, www.krisbradley.com.

Z Budapest

Zsuzsanna Emese Budapest is a Hungarian-born American feminist writer. She is the child of spiritual artists who made their living by creating home altars. Steeped in ancient mythology, Z has passed on magical knowledge in her books, fairy tales, poetry, invocations, and folk customs. Her work had ignited the Goddess movement; her works gave it content and practice. A master of rituals, she has seeded the women's mysteries globally. Find her books at zbudapest.com.

Raven Digitalis

Raven Digitalis is the author of *Shadow Magick Compendium, Planetary Spells & Rituals,* and *Goth Craft.* He is a Neopagan priest and cofounder of an Eastern Hellenistic coven and order called Opus Aima Obscuræ (OAO), and he is a radio and club DJ of Gothic and industrial music. Also trained in Georgian Witchcraft and Buddhist philosophy, Raven has been a Witch since 1999, a priest since 2003, a Freemason since 2012, and an empath all of his life. Raven holds a degree in anthropology from the University of Montana and is also a professional tarot reader.

Lupa

Lupa is the author of *New Paths to Animal Totems: Three Alternative Approaches to Creating Your Own Totemism* (Llewellyn, 2012) and *Plant and Fungus Totems: Connecting with Spirits of Field, Forest, and Garden* (Llewellyn, 2014).

Melanie Marquis

Melanie Marquis is the author of *A Witch's World of Magick* (Llewellyn, 2014), *The Witch's Bag of Tricks* (Llewellyn, 2011), and *Bugbug and the Ants* (Featherweight Press, 2013). See http://www.melaniemarquis.com and http://www.facebook.com/melaniemarquisauthor.

Mickie Mueller

Mickie Mueller is an award-winning and critically acclaimed artist of fantasy, fairy, and myth. She is an ordained Pagan minister and has studied natural magic, fairy magic, and Celtic tradition. She is also a Reiki healing master/teacher in the Usui Shiki Royoho Tradition. She enjoys creating magical art full of fairies, goddesses, and beings of folklore. She works primarily in a mix of colored pencil and watercolor infused with magical herbs corresponding to her subject matter. Mickie is the illustrator of *The Well Worn Path* and *The Hidden Path* decks, the writer/illustrator of *The Voice of the Trees: A Celtic Divination Oracle*, and the illustrator of *Mystical Cats Tarot*. Mickie is a regular article contributor to several of the Llewellyn annuals. Visit her online at www.mickiemuellerart.com.

Ashleen O'Gaea

Ashleen O'Gaea is an ordained Wiccan priestess and the author of several books about Wicca, ranging from the first-ever book for Wiccan families to a post-Arthurian fantasy, along with books for middle school and younger children. She shares a home with her husband and three affectionate cats, her favorite color is currently turquoise, and she takes her single malt neat. She's online at www.AshleenOGaea.com and on several Facebook pages, including O'Gaea the Writer and Adventure Wicca.

Christopher Penczak

Christopher Penczak is the cofounder of the Temple of Witchcraft, a system of training, a tradition, and a community rooted in the New England area and dedicated to the principles of Love, Will, and Wisdom. He is an award-winning author who draws upon classic occultism, folklore, and modern metaphysical thought, and his work includes *The Plant Spirit Familiar*, *The Mighty Dead*, *The Witch's Shield*, and the popular six-book Temple of Witchcraft series. Christopher works as a modern-day cunning man, using his skills and knowledge to teach, heal, and perform divination and rituals for those seeking aid. See www.christopherpenczak.com and www.templeofwitchcraft.org.

Gail Wood

Gail Wood is a Witch, priestess, and elder of the RavenMyst Circle in central New York. She is the author of *The Shamanic Witch*, articles, and two other books currently out of print. She can be seen (or at least read) on her blog at www.rowdygoddess.com.

Recommended Reading

The book lists I already gave you are just the tip of the iceberg. There are many, many wonderful books available on a range of topics having to do with Wicca, Witchcraft, Paganism, and beyond. Here are some of the ones you will find on my bookshelves; there are plenty more besides. If you only take away one suggestion from everything I have said, it is this: keep learning! And along with the titles already mentioned in chapter 11, these are a good place to start.

Bolen, Jean Shinoda. *Goddesses in Older Women: Archetypes in Women Over Fifty.* New York: Harper Collins, 2001.

Bonewits, Isaac. *Real Magic: An Introductory Treatise on the Basic Principles of Yellow Magic.* Boston: Red Wheel/Weiser, 1989.

Buckland, Raymond. *Buckland's Book of Gypsy Magic: Traveler's Stories, Spells & Healings.* San Francisco: Red Wheel/Weiser Books, 2010.

———. *Wicca for Life: The Way of the Craft—from Birth to Summerland.* New York: Citadel Press, 2001.

Cole, Jennifer. *Ceremonies of the Seasons: Exploring and Celebrating Nature's Eternal Cycle.* London: Duncan Baird Publishers, 2007.

Conner, Kerri. *Spells for Tough Times: Crafting Hope When Faced with Life's Thorniest Challenges.* Woodbury: Llewellyn, 2012.

Conway, D. J. *Magickal Mystical Creatures: Invite Their Powers into Your Life.* St. Paul: Llewellyn, 1996.

Cunningham, Scott. *Magical Herbalism: The Secret Craft of the Wise.* St. Paul: Llewellyn, 1982.

Digitalis, Raven. *Goth Craft: The Magickal Side of Dark Culture.* Woodbury: Llewellyn, 2007.

———. *Planetary Spells & Rituals: Practicing Dark & Light Magick Aligned with the Cosmic Bodies.* Woodbury: Llewellyn, 2010.

Dugan, Ellen. *The Enchanted Cat: Feline Fascinations, Spells & Magick.* Woodbury: Llewellyn, 2006.

———. *Garden Witchery: Magick from the Ground Up.* St. Paul: Llewellyn, 2003.

Dunwich, Gerina. *The Wicca Garden: A Modern Witch's Book of Magickal and Enchanted Herbs and Plants.* New York: Citadel Press, 1996.

Emoto, Masuru. *The Hidden Messages in Water.* New York: Atria Books, 2004.

Ferguson, Joy. *Magickal Weddings: Pagan Handfasting Traditions for Your Sacred Union.* Toronto: ECW Press, 2001.

Fitch, Ed. *Magical Rites from the Crystal Well.* St. Paul: Llewellyn, 1984, 2000.

Franklin, Anna. *A Romantic Guide to Handfasting: Rituals, Recipes & Lore.* St. Paul: Llewellyn, 2004.

Galenorn, Yasmine. *Embracing the Moon: A Witch's Guide to Ritual, Spellcraft, and Shadow Work.* St. Paul: Llewellyn, 1999.

Green, Marion. *A Witch Alone: Thirteen Moons to Master Natural Magic.* London: Thorsons, 1991.

Grimassi, Raven. *Old World Witchcraft: Ancient Ways for Modern Days.* San Francisco: Weiser, 2011.

————. *Spirit of the Witch: Religion & Spirituality in Contemporary Witchcraft*. St. Paul: Llewellyn, 2003.

Harrison, Karen. *The Herbal Alchemist's Handbook: A Grimoire of Philtres, Elixirs, Oils, Incense, and Formulas for Ritual Use*. San Francisco: Red Wheel/Weiser, 2001.

Henes, Donna. *The Queen of Myself: Stepping into Sovereignty in Midlife*. Brooklyn: Monarch Press, 2005.

Holland, Eileen. *The Wicca Handbook*. York Beach: Samuel Weiser, 2000.

———— and Cerelia. *A Witch's Book of Answers*. York Beach: Red Wheel/Weiser, 2003.

Hopman, Ellen Evert. *A Druid's Herbal for the Sacred Year*. Rochester: Destiny Books, 1995.

Howard, Michael. *Modern Wicca: A History from Gerald Gardner to the Present*. Woodbury: Llewellyn, 2009.

Illes, Judika. *Encyclopedia of 500 Spells: The Ultimate Reference Book for the Magical Arts*. New York: HarperOne, 2009.

————. *Encyclopedia of Mystics, Saints & Sages: A Guide to Asking for Protection, Wealth, Happiness, and Everything Else!* New York: HarperCollins, 2011.

————. *Encyclopedia of Spirits: The Ultimate Guide to the Magic of Fairies, Genies, Demons, Ghosts, Gods & Goddesses*. New York: HarperCollins, 2009.

Kaldera, Raven, and Tannin Schwartzstein. *Handfasting and Wedding Rituals: Inviting Hera's Blessing*. St. Paul: Llewellyn, 2003.

Kynes, Sandra. *A Year of Ritual: Sabbats & Esbats for Solitaries & Covens*. St. Paul: Llewellyn, 2004.

MacLir, Alferian Gwydion. *Wandlore: The Art of Crafting the Ultimate Magical Tool*. Woodbury: Llewellyn, 2011.

McCoy, Edain. *Celtic Myth & Magick: Harnessing the Power of the Gods and Goddesses*. St. Paul: Llewellyn, 1995.

———. *The Healing Power of Faery: Working with Elementals and Nature Spirits to Soothe the Body and Soul*. St. Paul: Llewellyn, 2008.

Morningstar, Sally. *The Art of Wiccan Healing: A Practical Guide*. Carlsbad: Hay House, 2005.

Morrison, Dorothy. *Everyday Sun Magic: Spells & Rituals for Radiant Living*. Woodbury: Llewellyn, 2005.

Peschel, Lisa. *A Practical Guide to the Runes: Their Uses in Divination and Magick*. St. Paul: Llewellyn, 1989.

Rhea, Lady Mauve. *Handfasted and Heartjoined: Rituals for Uniting a Couple's Hearts and Lives*. New York: Citadel Press, 2001.

River, Jade. *Tying the Knot: A Gender-Neutral Guide to Handfastings or Weddings for Pagans and Goddess Worshipers*. Cottage Grove: Creatrix Resource Library LLC, 2004.

SpiderHawk, Vila. *Hidden Passages: Tales to Honor the Crones*. Niceville: Spilled Candy Books, 2006.

Telesco, Patricia. *Advanced Wicca: Exploring Deeper Levels of Spiritual Skills and Masterful Magick*. New York: Citadel Press, 2000.

———. *Exploring Candle Magick: Candle Spells, Charms, Rituals, and Divinations*. Franklin Lakes: New Page Books, 2001.

———. *Your Book of Shadows: How to Write Your Own Magickal Spells*. New York: Citadel Press, 1999.

Trobe, Kala. *The Witch's Guide to Life*. St. Paul: Llewellyn, 2003.

Webster, Richard. *Candle Magic for Beginners: The Easiest Magic You Can Do*. St. Paul: Llewellyn, 2004.

Whitehurst, Tess. *The Good Energy Book: Creating Harmony and Balance for Yourself and Your Home*. Woodbury: Llewellyn, 2012.

————. *The Magic of Flowers: A Guide to Their Metaphysical Uses & Properties*. Woodbury: Llewellyn, 2013.

Wood, Gail. *Rituals of the Dark Moon: 13 Lunar Rites for a Magical Path*. St. Paul: Llewellyn, 2001.

Worwood, Valerie Ann. *The Complete Book of Essential Oils & Aromatherapy*. San Rafael: New World Library, 1991.

I also highly recommend the various Llewellyn annuals and almanacs, as well as the fabulous magazines put out by BBI Media (including *Witches & Pagans*, in which I have a regular column).

GET MORE AT LLEWELLYN.COM

Visit us online to browse hundreds of our books and decks, plus sign up to receive our e-newsletters and exclusive online offers.

- Free tarot readings • Spell-a-Day • Moon phases
- Recipes, spells, and tips • Blogs • Encyclopedia
- Author interviews, articles, and upcoming events

GET SOCIAL WITH LLEWELLYN

Find us on   🐦 @LlewellynBooks

www.Facebook.com/LlewellynBooks

GET BOOKS AT LLEWELLYN

LLEWELLYN ORDERING INFORMATION

Order online: Visit our website at www.llewellyn.com to select your books and place an order on our secure server.

Order by phone:
- Call toll free within the US at 1-877-NEW-WRLD (1-877-639-9753)
- We accept VISA, MasterCard, American Express, and Discover.

Order by mail:
Send the full price of your order (MN residents add 6.875% sales tax) in US funds plus postage and handling to: Llewellyn Worldwide, 2143 Wooddale Drive, Woodbury, MN 55125-2989

POSTAGE AND HANDLING

STANDARD (US):(Please allow 12 business days)
$30.00 and under, add $6.00.
$30.01 and over, FREE SHIPPING.

CANADA:
We cannot ship to Canada. Please shop your local bookstore or Amazon Canada.

INTERNATIONAL:
Customers pay the actual shipping cost to the final destination, which includes tracking information.

Visit us online for more shipping options. Prices subject to change.

FREE CATALOG!

To order, call
1-877-
NEW-WRLD
ext. 8236
or visit our
website

To Write to the Author

If you wish to contact the author or would like more information about this book, please write to the author in care of Llewellyn Worldwide and we will forward your request. Both the author and the publisher appreciate hearing from you and learning of your enjoyment of this book and how it has helped you. Llewellyn Worldwide cannot guarantee that every letter written to the author can be answered, but all will be forwarded. Please write to:

Deborah Blake
℅ Llewellyn Worldwide
2143 Wooddale Drive
Woodbury, MN 55125-2989

Please enclose a self-addressed stamped envelope for reply
or $1.00 to cover costs. If outside the USA, enclose
an international postal reply coupon.

Many of Llewellyn's authors have websites with additional information and resources. For more information, please visit our website:

www.llewellyn.com